REFLECTIONS

on the

Catechism

of the

Catholic Church

REFLECTIONS

on the

Catechism

of the

Catholic Church

Compiled by
Reverend James P. Socias

Midwest Theological Forum
Chicago

This edition of *Reflections on the Catechism of the Catholic Church is* published by :

Midwest Theological Forum
1410 W. Lexington St.
Chicago, IL 60607

The **Midwest Theological Forum** is an educational service organized by priests of the Prelature of Opus Dei and other diocesan priests.

Reprinted with permission from L'Osservatore Romano (English edition)

ISBN: 093393267-7

Printed in the United States of America

Contents

PART TWO

Reflections on the *Catechism of the Catholic Church*

III. *The divine economy interwoven
      through new catechetical work* 75
      Christoph Schönborn, O. P.
      Auxiliary Bishop of Vienna, Austria

IV. *Eastern tradition reflected
      in new catechism's spirituality* 85
      Guy-Paul Noujeim
      Maronite Patriarchal Vicar of Sarba-Kesrouan, Lebanon

V.   *Catechism responds to desire
      and needs of Church today* 91
      Cardinal Carlo M. Martini, S.J.
      Archbishop of Milan, Italy

VI. *Catechism offers prospects
      for ecumenical reflection* 97
      Fr. Max Thurian
      International Theological Commission

APPENDICES

APPENDICES

Reports on the Seminar on the *Catechism of the Catholic Church* and the catechetical apostolate Thursday, April 29, 1993

Foreword

On December 7, 1992 I was privileged to be present in the Sala Clementina when the Holy Father presented the *Catechism of the Catholic Church*. It was seven years earlier to the day that the Pope accepted the recommendation of the 1985 Extraordinary Synod of Bishops concerning a catechism. On that occasion John Paul II said: "The desire expressed to prepare a compendium or catechism of all Catholic doctrine to serve as a point of reference for catechisms or compendia on this theme in all the particular churches . . . responds to a real need both of the universal Church and of the particular churches." (*Address at the Closing of the Extraordinary Synod*, December 7, 1985, n.6)

In accepting the *Catechism* on behalf of my brother Bishops around the world, I mentioned that it will be up to us and our helpers to translate its proclamation of the faith of the Church into the many cultural languages of the human communities from which we come and into which we have been sent as evangelizers and catechists. Recalling the reminder of Paul VI in *Evangelii Nuntiandi* that the Church is both an evangelized and an evangelizing community, I said then and I repeat now that "in carrying out the mission of proclamation, this new *Catechism of the Catholic Church* will be an invaluable and rich resource, as well as a clear norm, as we strive to transmit the Gospel to all the nations and as we are constantly evangelized ourselves."

This book collects a series of reflections on the *Catechism* written by especially qualified authors and originally published in *L'Osservatore Romano*. No reflection or series of reflections can be a substitute for the text itself, as the writers of these commentaries say again and again. These reflections are accompanied by some statements of the Holy Father himself as he speaks of the importance of the *Catechism*. The credibility of anyone else's comments can be measured by the

Pope's words. Three brief quotations from the Pope's statements will suffice here, their context easily found in the complete texts contained in this book.

Regarding the authority of the *Catechism,* in the Apostolic Constitution on its publication the Holy Father said that the *Catechism* "is a statement of the Church's faith and of Catholic doctrine, attested to or illumined by Sacred Scripture, Apostolic Tradition and the Church's Magisterium. I declare it to be a valid and legitimate instrument for ecclesial communion and a sure norm for teaching the faith." *(Fidei Depositum,* October 11, 1992, n.4)

Regarding the intended audience of the *Catechism* the Pope has stated that "the new *Catechism* is given to the Pastors and faithful because, like every genuine catechism, it serves to educate people in the faith which the Catholic Church professes and proclaims. However, it is a gift for all: *in fact, it is addressed to all and must reach everyone . . . .* It *cannot be considered merely as a stage preceding the drafting of local catechisms,* but is destined for all the faithful who have the capacity to read, understand and assimilate it in their Christian living." *(Address at a special audience to participants in a workshop on preparing local catechisms,* sponsored by the Congregation for the Clergy, April 29, 1993, n.5). Even more, the *Catechism* "is offered to every individual who asks us to give an account of the hope that is in us (cf. 1 Pt 3: 15) and who wants to know what the Catholic Church believes." *(Fidei Depositum,* n. 4).

Regarding its purpose, in the annual letter on the occasion of Holy Thursday, John Paul II told his brother priests that "this *Catechism* is given to us as *a sure point of reference* for fulfilling the mission, entrusted to us in the Sacrament of Orders, of proclaiming the 'Good News' to all people *in the name of Christ and of the Church . . . .* Indeed, in this summary of the deposit of faith, we can find an *authentic and sure norm* for teaching

Catholic doctrine, for catechetical activity among the Christian people, for that 'new evangelization' of which today's world has such immense need." (Letter, April 8, 1993, n.2)

Indeed, the world needs a new evangelization. The Gospel of St. Matthew ends with the apostolic command: "All authority in heaven and on earth has been given to me. Go therefore and make disciples of all nations, baptizing them in the name of the Father and of the Son and of the Holy Spirit, teaching them to observe all that I have commanded you; and lo, I am with you always, to the close of the age (Matthew 28: 18-20).

The apostolic command has reached from the heart of Christ to the hearts of all his followers, to the heart of each one of us: bishop, priest, catechist, parent. The Bride has pondered these words of her Spouse for almost two millennia, as she keeps her youthfulness which is a share in the eternity of God. She has pondered them anew as we approach the end of the millennium and has proclaimed them: in the Decree *Ad Gentes* of Vatican II, in the Apostolic Exhortation *Evangelii Nuntiandi* of Paul VI, in the Encyclical *Redemptoris Missio* of John Paul II. And now in the *Catechism of the Catholic Church*.

As the Apostles waited for the Holy Spirit, they were all together (cf. Acts 2: 1) and they were with Mary, the mother of Jesus (cf. Acts 1: 14).

We also need to be with Mary, the mother of Jesus and Mother of the Church. It is to her that the Holy Father entrusts the *Catechism of the Catholic Church* when he wrote in the Apostolic Constitution of promulgation: "I beseech the Blessed Virgin Mary, Mother of the Incarnate Word and Mother of the Church, to support with her powerful intercession the catechetical work of the entire Church at every level, at this time when she is called to a new effort of evangelization. May the light of the true faith free humanity from ignorance and slavery to sin in order to lead it to the only freedom worthy of the name (cf.

Jn 8: 32); that of life in Jesus Christ under the guidance of the Holy Spirit, here below and in the kingdom of heaven in the fullness of the blessed vision of God face to face (cf. 1 Cor 13: 12; 2 Cor 5: 6-8) !" (*Fidei Depositum,* n.5).

Bernard Cardinal Law
Archbishop of Boston

PART ONE:
Addresses from
Pope John Paul II

I

Apostolic Constitution
FIDEI DEPOSITUM

Pope John Paul II
Sunday, October 11, 1992

To my Venerable Brothers the Cardinals, to the Archbishops, Bishops, Priests, Deacons and all the People of God,

1. Introduction

Guarding the deposit of faith is the mission which the Lord has entrusted to his Church and which she fulfils in every age. The Second Vatican Ecumenical Council, which was opened 30 years ago by my predecessor Pope John XXIII, of happy memory, had as its intention and purpose to highlight the Church's apostolic and pastoral mission, and by making the truth of the Gospel shine forth, to lead all people to seek and receive Christ's love which surpasses all knowledge (cf. Eph 3: 19).

The principal task entrusted to the Council by Pope John XXIII was to guard and present better the precious deposit of Christian doctrine in order to make it more accessible to the Christian faithful and to all people of good will. For this reason the Council was not first of all to condemn the errors of the time, but above all to strive calmly to show the strength and beauty of the doctrine of the faith. "Illumined by the light of this Council", the Pope said, "the Church . . . will become greater in spiritual riches and, gaining the strength of new energies therefrom, she will look to the future without fear . . .. Our duty is . . . to dedicate ourselves with an earnest will and without fear to that work which our era demands of us, thus pursuing the path which the Church has followed for 20 centuries."[1]

With the help of God, the Council Fathers in four years of work were able to produce a considerable collection of doctrinal statements and pastoral norms which were presented to the whole Church. There the Pastors and Christian faithful find directives for that "renewal of thought, action, practices and moral virtue, of joy and hope, which was the very purpose of the Council."[2]

After its conclusion the Council did not cease to inspire the Church's life. In 1985 I was able to assert: "For me, then—who had the special grace of participating in it and actively collaborating in its development—Vatican II has always been, and especially during these years of my Pontificate, the constant reference point of my every pastoral action, in the conscious commitment to implement its directives concretely and faithfully at the level of each Church and the whole Church."[3]

In this spirit, on January 25, 1985 I convoked an Extraordinary Assembly of the Synod of Bishops for the 20th anniversary of the close of the Council. The purpose of this assembly was to celebrate the graces and spiritual fruits of Vatican II, to study its teaching in greater depth in order the better to adhere to it and to promote knowledge and application of it.

On that occasion the Synod Fathers stated: "Very many have expressed the desire that a catechism or compendium of all Catholic doctrine regarding both faith and morals be composed, that it might be, as it were, a point of reference for the catechisms or compendiums that are prepared in various regions. The presentation of doctrine must be biblical and liturgical. It must be sound doctrine suited to the present life of Christians."[4] After the Synod ended, I made this desire my own, considering it as "fully responding to a real need both of the universal Church and of the particular Churches."[5]

For this reason we thank the Lord wholeheartedly on this day when we can offer the entire Church this "reference text" entitled the *Catechism of the Catholic Church,* for a catechesis renewed at the living sources of the faith!

Following the renewal of the Liturgy and the new codification of the canon law of the Latin Church and that of the Oriental Catholic Churches, this *Catechism* will make a very important contribution to that work of renewing the whole life of the Church, as desired and begun by the Second Vatican Council.

2. The process and spirit of drafting the text

The *Catechism of the Catholic Church* is the result of very extensive collaboration: it was prepared over six years of intense work done in a spirit of complete openness and fervent zeal.

In 1986 I entrusted a commission of 12 Cardinals and Bishops, chaired by Cardinal Joseph Ratzinger, with the task of preparing a draft of the catechism requested by the Synod Fathers. An editorial committee of seven diocesan Bishops, experts in theology and catechesis, assisted the commission in its work.

The commission, charged with giving directives and with overseeing the course of the work, attentively followed all the stages in editing the nine subsequent drafts. The editorial committee, for its part, assumed responsibility for writing the text, making the emendations requested by the commission and examining the observations of numerous theologians, exegetes and catechists, and above all, of the Bishops of the whole world, in order to improve the text. The committee was a place of fruitful and enriching exchanges of opinion to ensure the unity and homogeneity of the text.

The project was the object of extensive consultation among all Catholic Bishops, their Episcopal Conferences or Synods, and of theological and catechetical institutes. As a whole, it received a broadly favorable acceptance on the part of the Episcopate. It can be said that this *Catechism* is the result of the collaboration of the whole Episcopate of the Catholic Church, who generously accepted my invitation to share responsibility for an enterprise which directly concerns the life of the Church. This response elicits in me a deep feeling of joy, because the harmony of so many voices truly expresses what could be called the "symphony" of the faith. The achievement of this *Catechism* thus reflects the collegial nature of the Episcopate: it testifies to the Church's catholicity.

3. Arrangement of the material

A catechism should faithfully and systematically present the teaching of Sacred Scripture, the living Tradition of the Church and the authentic Magisterium, as well as the spiritual heritage of the Fathers and the Church's saints, to allow for a better knowledge of the Christian mystery and for enlivening the faith of the People of God. It should take into account the doctrinal statements which down the centuries the Holy Spirit has intimated to his Church. It should also help illumine with the light of faith the new situations and problems which had not yet emerged in the past.

The *Catechism* will thus contain the new and the old (cf. Mt 13: 52), because the faith is always the same yet the source of ever new light.

To respond to this twofold demand, the *Catechism of the Catholic Church* on the one hand repeats the "old", traditional order already followed by the *Catechism* of St. Pius V, arranging the material in four parts: the *Creed,* the *Sacred Liturgy,* with pride of place given to the sacraments, the *Christian way of life,* explained beginning with the Ten Commandments, and finally, *Christian prayer.* At the same time, however, the contents are often expressed in a "new" way in order to respond to the questions of our age.

The four parts are related one to the other: the Christian mystery is the object of faith (First Part); it is celebrated and communicated in liturgical actions (Second Part), it is present to enlighten and sustain the children of God in their actions (Third Part); it is the basis for our prayer, the privileged expression of which is the *Our Father,* and it represents the object of our supplication, our praise and our intercession (fourth part).

The Liturgy itself is prayer; the confession of faith finds its proper place in the celebration of worship. Grace, the fruit of the sacraments, is the irreplaceable condition for Christian living, just as participation in the Church's liturgy requires faith. If faith is not expressed in works, it is dead (cf. Jas 2: 14-16) and cannot bear fruit unto eternal life.

In reading the *Catechism of the Catholic Church* we can perceive the wondrous unity of the mystery of God, his saving will, as well as the central place of Jesus Christ, the only-begotten Son of God, sent by the Father, made man in the womb of the Blessed Virgin

Mary by the power of the Holy Spirit, to be our Saviour. Having died and risen, Christ is always present in his Church, especially in the sacraments; he is the source of our faith, the model of Christian conduct and the Teacher of our prayer.

4. The doctrinal value of the text

The *Catechism of the Catholic Church,* which I approved last 25 June and the publication of which I today order by virtue of my Apostolic Authority, is a statement of the Church's faith and of Catholic doctrine, attested to or illumined by Sacred Scripture, Apostolic Tradition and the Church's Magisterium. I declare it to be a valid and legitimate instrument for ecclesial communion and a sure norm for teaching the faith. May it serve the renewal to which the Holy Spirit ceaselessly calls the Church of God, the Body of Christ, on her pilgrimage to the undiminished light of the kingdom!

The approval and publication of the *Catechism of the Catholic Church* represents a service which the Successor of Peter wishes to offer to the Holy Catholic Church, and to all the particular Churches in peace and communion with the Apostolic See: the service that is, of supporting and confirming the faith of all the Lord Jesus' disciples (cf. Lk 22: 32), as well as of strengthening the bonds of unity in the same apostolic faith.

Therefore, I ask the Church's Pastors and the Christian faithful to receive this *Catechism* in a spirit of communion and to use it assiduously in fulfilling their mission of proclaiming the faith and calling people to the Gospel life. This *Catechism* is given to them that it may be a sure and authentic reference text for teaching Catholic doctrine and particularly for preparing local catechisms. It is also offered to all the faithful who wish to deepen their knowledge of the unfathomable riches of salvation (cf. Jn 8: 32). It is meant to support ecumenical efforts that are moved by the holy desire for the unity of all Christians, showing carefully the content and wondrous harmony of the Catholic faith. The *Catechism of the Catholic Church,* lastly, is offered to every individual who asks us to give an account of the hope that is in us (cf. 1 Pt 3: 15) and who wants to know what the Catholic Church believes.

This *Catechism* is not intended to replace the local catechisms duly approved by the ecclesiastical authorities, the diocesan Bishops and the Episcopal Conferences, especially if they have been approved by the Apostolic See. It is meant to encourage and assist in the writing of new local catechisms, which must take into account various situations and cultures, while carefully preserving the unity of faith and fidelity to Catholic doctrine.

5. Conclusion

At the conclusion of this document presenting the *Catechism of the Catholic Church*, I beseech the Blessed Virgin Mary, Mother of the Incarnate Word and Mother of the Church, to support with her powerful intercession the catechetical work of the entire Church on every level, at this time when she is called to a new effort of evangelization. May the light of the true faith free humanity from ignorance and slavery to sin in order to lead it to the only freedom worthy of the name (cf. Jn 8: 32): that of life in Jesus Christ under the guidance of the Holy Spirit, here below and in the kingdom of heaven, in the fullness of the blessed vision of God face to face (cf. 1 Cor 13: 12; 2 Cor 5: 6-8)!

Given on October 11, 1992, the thirtieth anniversary of the opening of the Second Vatican Ecumenical Council, in the fourteenth year of my Pontificate.

Joannes Paulus pp. I

Notes

1   John XXIII, Opening Address to the Second Vatican Ecumenical Council, October 11, 1962: *AAS* 54 (1962), pp. 788, 791.
2   Paul VI, Closing Address to the Second Vatican Ecumenical Council, December 8, 1965: *AAS* 58 (1966), pp. 7-8.
3   John Paul II, Address of January 25, 1985: *L'Osservatore Romano,* January 27, 1985.
4   Final Report of the Extraordinary Synod, December 7, 1985, II, B, a, n. 4: *Enchiridion Vaticanum,* vol. 9, p. 1758, n. 1797.
5   John Paul II, Address at the closing of the Extraordinary Synod, December 7, 1985, n. 6: *AAS* 78 (1986), p. 435.

II

New Catechism to serve
Church renewal

Pope John Paul II
Sunday, November 15, 1992

Dear Brothers and Sisters,

1. Today I would like to share with you *an event of great importance* for the life of the Church. I am referring to the publication of the *Catechism of the Catholic Church* which I approved last June. It will be accompanied by an official presentation which will include a *ceremonial* act on December 7 and a *liturgical celebration* on December 8, followed by a press conference on December 9.

It will be an event of historic importance because the new *Catechism* is not just another book of theology or catechesis, but rather a general reference text for the catechetical activity of the whole People of God.

The context in which it can be situated is that delineated by the Second Vatican Ecumenical Council when the Church expressed the desire to "hear the word of God with reverence" *(Dei Verbum,* n. 1) in order to understand herself ever better and to enter into dialogue with the people of our times. In that bright conciliar spring time, under the action of the Holy Spirit, the Church drew from her treasury "new things as well as old" (Mt 13: 52).

The new *Catechism* represents a qualified and authoritative tool for mediating the Church's self-knowledge, strongly anchored in the one and unchanging truth of the Gospel, but also attentive to the "signs of the times" and totally committed to the new evangelization and human development.

2. I am certain that the publication of the new *Catechism* will be a valuable opportunity for all the faithful to strengthen their faith and increase their missionary spirit, thus fostering an authentic renewal of the Church.

In fact, faith demands that *people listen to the word of God* authoritatively proclaimed by the Apostles and their successors. It is not a vague, subjective attitude but rather an assent of mind and heart to the revealed Truth, or better, to Christ himself, the "Way, the Truth and the Life" (Jn 14: 6).

When faith is accepted and lived it impels believers to *proclaim and witness the "good news" of the Gospel* to all people. As the Third Millennium of the Christian era rapidly draws near, the Church feels challenged more greatly than ever by Jesus' missionary mandate: "Go and teach all nations" (Mt 28: 19).

The "*Catechism* of the Universal Church" is meant to be at the service of that renewal of faith and missionary spirit in believers who are committed to living out their Baptism in the contemporary world.

3. In the recitation of the Angelus let us invoke Mary, Mother of the Church and Star of Evangelization, that she may obtain for the whole Christian community the grace of a docile, sincere and energetic acceptance of this new tool of faith which we hope will bear abundant fruit in the maturation of the People of God and the evangelization of the world.

III

Catechism expresses 'symphony' of faith

Pope John Paul II
November 29, 1992
First Sunday of Advent

Dear Brothers and Sisters,

1. Today is the beginning of the liturgical season of Advent, during which we prepare to relive the mystery of the Redeemer's birth: such an ancient event, but always mysteriously new.

It is *ancient* because it is rooted in God's eternal plan which, although it was fulfilled historically almost 2,000 years ago, was prepared from the dawn of creation. At the same time, it is an ever *new* event because from generation to generation it releases its inexhaustible redemptive energy as we wait for Christ to return in glory.

In the light of this mystery, human history shows a profound unity over and above everyday difficulties, and human beings are called to shape it in a responsible, active dialogue with divine Providence.

I truly hope that Advent, a time of waiting, listening and hoping, will be a favorable time for all believers to strengthen their faith and confirm their commitment to give a consistent witness of their Christian life.

2. In this context of spiritual renewal we can also see the publication of the new *Catechism of the Catholic Church*. It is the result of the fruitful collaboration among the diocesan Bishops

of all continents, in close communion with the Successor of Peter.

It originated from a recommendation made by the Assembly of the Synod of Bishops in 1985. At that time many Synod Fathers expressed their desire for a compendium of Catholic doctrine which could serve as a point of reference for the catechisms prepared in the various regions (cf. *Relatio finalis,* II, B, 4).

It was a useful suggestion, which I gladly accepted, creating a commission to see to its realization. Prelates from throughout the world were thus able actively to help in editing the definitive text which I had the joy of approving on June 25, and which I promulgated on October 11, the 30th anniversary of the opening of the Second Vatican Ecumenical Council.

3. Looking at the progress that has been made, I give thanks to the Lord for the wonderful "symphony" of faith which has been shown once again, and I express my wish that the new *Catechism* will bear abundant fruit in the whole Church.

I entrust this valuable instrument of the new evangelization to Mary, the immaculate Virgin, the sublime example of the People of God on their "pilgrimage of faith" *(Lumen Gentium,* n. 58; cf. *Redemptoris Mater,* n. 2), who knows quite well the difficulties and temptations which ecclesial communities are subject to in our day.

By her maternal intercession may Mary obtain the grace of a renewed impetus to giving the world an account of the hope that is in us (cf. 1 Pt 3: 15).

Mary, Help of Christians, pray for us!

IV

Catechesis should have an impact on the daily life of every Christian community

Pope John Paul II
December 6, 1992
Second Sunday of Advent

Dear Brothers and Sisters,

1. The liturgical season of Advent we are living through helps us to have a renewed awareness of the *eschatological dimension of the Christian life.*

The Church here below is a "pilgrim people" (cf. *Lumen Gentium,* n. 48). The goal she is striving for is Christ's return in glory. He, who already came in the humility of the Incarnation, will come again at the end of time as the Lord and Judge of history. This is why the prayer of believers always pulsates with Advent longing: "Come, Lord Jesus—*Marana tha*"(Rv 22: 20).

In this confident and watchful expectation, the Church does not tire of telling the world the reason for her hope, *Christ the Redeemer of man.*

2. To make Christ better known and his message generously welcomed, she wants to offer the new *Catechism of the Catholic Church,* which will officially be made public over the next few days: *tomorrow,* December 7, during a "celebration"; *Tuesday,* the Solemnity of the Immaculate Conception, with a Eucharistic celebration in the Basilica of St. Mary Major; and *Wednesday,*

December 9, during a special meeting with journalists and those who work in social communications.

This new text represents *a privileged tool* and *a pressing invitation* to an appropriate Gospel formation in order to begin the new evangelization with firm conviction and apostolic foresight.

Hence the *urgent need for catechesis,* called to break the bread of God's word, thus fostering an ever deeper understanding of it in regard to the challenges of our time.

This catechesis is certainly not exhausted in merely transmitting ideas. Its task is "to advance in fullness and to nourish day by day the Christian life of the faithful, young and old", so that the believer may be "impregnated" by the mystery of Christ, and thus learn ever better "to think like him, to judge like him, to act in conformity with his commandments, to hope as he invites us to" *(Catechesi Tradendæ,* n. 20).

The new *"Catechism"*, a reference point for the catechesis of the Christian communities spread throughout the world, will provide a sure path in this direction.

3. Let us pray to the Blessed Virgin to give the whole Church a new impetus in the task of spreading the Good News of salvation.

May Mary, whom the Gospel presents to us as the woman who listens, she who "treasured in her heart" and reflected on all the events and words by which God revealed himself (cf. Lk 2: 19, 51), enable us, especially in this season of Advent, to listen with docility and willingly to the word of the Lord, so that with a new heart we can live the mystery of the Redeemer's birth.

V

Catechism is truly a gift to the Church

Pope John Paul II
Sunday, December 7, 1992

In a special ceremony His Holiness officially presented the new Catechism of the Catholic Church.

Your Eminences,
Venerable Brothers,
Representatives of the Peoples,
Dear Faithful,
Authorities and Citizens of every part of the world,

1. The holy Church of God rejoices today because, as a special gift of divine providence, she can solemnly celebrate the promulgation of the new *"Catechism"*, presenting it officially to the faithful of the whole world. I give great thanks to the God of heaven and earth because he has allowed me to experience with you an event of incomparable richness and importance.

A cause for profound joy for the universal Church is this *gift which the heavenly Father gives to his children today,* offering them with this text the possibility of knowing better, in the light of his Spirit, the breadth and length and height and depth of Christ's love (cf. Eph 3: 19).

Benedicamus Domino!

2. I am deeply grateful to all those who collaborated in any way in the drafting of the *Catechism of the Catholic Church.* In particular I cannot fail to congratulate and rejoice with the members of the *Editorial Commission* and *Committee,* who during the course of these six years have worked in a unity of sentiment and intention

under the wise guidance of their President, Cardinal Joseph Ratzinger. From my heart I thank all of you individually.

Your concern to explain the contents of the faith in a way that conforms to biblical truth, to the Church's genuine Tradition and in particular to the teaching of the Second Vatican Council; your effort to highlight what is basic and essential in the Christian message; your commitment to express the perennial Catholic truth anew in a language which better responds to the demands of today's world, are all crowned with success today.

Your tireless work, sustained by the charity of Christ which "impels us" (2 Cor 5: 14) to be faithful and courageous witnesses of his Word, made possible an undertaking which, at the beginning and even during the process, seemed to quite a few people absolutely impossible.

Desire of Special Assembly of Synod of Bishops

3. I set the work in motion, gladly acceding to the request of the Synod Fathers who had been convoked in 1985 to celebrate the 20th anniversary of the close of the Second Vatican Council. Indeed, in that request I recognized the desire to fulfil once again, in a renewed manner, Christ's perennial command: *"Euntes ergo, docete omnes gentes . . . docentes eos servare omnia quæcumque mandavi vobis"* (Mt 28: 19-20).

The *Catechism of the Catholic Church* is a qualified, authoritative instrument which the Church's Pastors desired first of all for themselves, as a valuable help in fulfilling the mission they have received from Christ to proclaim and witness the Good News to all people.

4. The publication of the text must certainly be counted among the major events of the Church's recent history. It *is a precious gift* because it faithfully reiterates the Christian doctrine of all times: it is *a rich gift* due to the topics treated with care and depth; it is *an opportune gift,* given the demands and needs of the modern age.

Most of all, it is *a true gift,* a gift, that is, which presents the Truth revealed by God in Christ and entrusted by him to his Church. The *Catechism* explains this Truth in the light of the Vatican

Council as it is *believed, celebrated, lived and prayed* by the Church and does so with the intention of fostering unfailing adherence to the Person of Christ.

Such a service to the Truth fills the Church with gratitude and joy, and imparts to her new courage to fulfil her mission in the world.

5. Furthermore, the *Catechism* is *a gift deeply rooted in the past.* Drawing abundantly on sacred Scripture and the inexhaustible apostolic Tradition, it collects, summarizes and transmits that incomparable richness which, despite dificulties and even differences, throughout 20 centuries of history has become the Church's ancient but ever new patrimony. Thus once again the Bride of Christ jealously fulfils her mission to guard the precious treasure which comes from on high and diligently works to make it bear fruit. Nothing ever changes in the eternal Catholic doctrine. Whatever was fundamental and essential in it still remains.

However, the living treasure of the past is explained and formulated in a new manner with a view to a greater fidelity to the integral truth about God and mankind, in the awareness that "the deposit or the truths of faith are one thing, and the way in which they are explained is something different, although their meaning and profound sense are always the same" (Vatican Council I, Dogmatic Constitution *Dei Filius,* chapter 4).

A harmonious synthesis of the Church's tradition

Therefore, this compendium of Catholic faith and morals is *a privileged gift* in which we have a convergence and collection in a harmonious synthesis of the Church's past, with her tradition her history of listening, proclaiming, celebrating and witnessing to the Word, with her Councils, doctors and saints.

Thus through successive generations, resounds the enduring and ever timely evangelical Magisterium of Christ, light of mankind for 20 centuries.

6. The *Catechism* is *a gift for the Church's present.* The bond with what is essential and venerable in the Church's past allows her to fulfil her mission among human beings today.

With a renewed self-awareness coming from the light of the Spirit, in this authoritative text the Church presents to her children the mystery of Christ in which the splendor of the Father is reflected.

It is the Church which expresses and implements, through this appropriate instrument, her constant desire and tireless search to rejuvenate her own countenance, so that the face of Christ, the one who is eternally young, can better appear in all its infinite beauty.

Thus she fulfils her mission to *know* ever more deeply, in order to *witness* to in its harmonious whole, the unfathomable riches of that Word which she serves. "She teaches only what has been handed on to her. At the divine command and with the help of the Holy Spirit, she listens to this devotedly, guards it with dedication and expounds it faithfully. All that she proposes for belief as being divinely revealed is drawn from this single deposit of faith" (Vatican II, *Dei Verbum,* n. 10).

7. Last of all, the *Catechism* is *a gift looking to the future.* From the meditative reflection on the mystery of Christ springs a courageous, generous teaching which the Church addresses to the future opening onto the third millennium.

It is not easy to see what developments this *Catechism* will bring about. However, it is certain that, with the grace of God and the good will of the Pastors and faithful, it could be a valuable, fruitful instrument for deeper knowledge and an authentic spiritual and moral renewal.

Conscious adherence to revealed doctrine, genuine and entire, which the *Catechism* presents in synthesis, will not fail to foster the progressive fulfillment of the plan of God who wants "everyone to be saved and to come to knowledge of the truth" (1 Tm 2: 4).

A gift to all Christians and all people of good will

8. *Unity in the truth:* this is the mission Christ entrusted to his Church, for which she works actively, invoking it first and foremost of him who can do all things and who, when his passion

and resurrection were imminent, first prayed to the Father that all believers might be "one" (Jn 17: 21).

Once again, through the gift of this *Catechism*, it is made clear that this mysterious, visible union *cannot be pursued without an identity of faith,* a sharing in the sacramental life, the resulting consistency in moral life and continuous, fervent personal and communal prayer.

Outlining Catholic doctrinal identity the *Catechism* can be a loving appeal even to those who are not part of the Catholic community. May they understand that this instrument does not limit but rather broadens the field of unity in multiplicity, offering new momentum on the path towards that fullness of communion which reflects and in some way anticipates the total unity of the heavenly city "in which truth reigns, charity is law and whose extension is eternity" (St. Augustine, *Epist. 138,* n. 3).

9. *A gift for everyone:* this is what the new *Catechism* is meant to be. In regard to this text, no one should feel a stranger, excluded or distant. In fact, it is addressed to everyone because it concerns the Lord of all, Jesus Christ, the one who proclaims and is proclaimed, the Awaited, the Teacher and the Model of every proclamation. It seeks to respond to and satisfy the needs of all those who, in their conscious or unconscious search for truth and certitude, seek God "even perhaps grope for him, though indeed he is not far from any one of us" (Acts 17: 27).

People of today and of all times *need Christ:* through many, sometimes incomprehensible ways, they seek him insistently, invoke him constantly, desire him ardently.

Guided by the Spirit, may they find him, too, by means of this instrument, the *Catechism.*

10. In order to bring that about, all of us, particularly Pastors of the holy People of God, must work together.

Just as the broad, fruitful cooperation of the Episcopate was fundamental in drafting the *Catechism of the Catholic Church, so* too for its use, implementation and effectiveness, the contribution of the Bishops, teachers of the faith in the Church, will above all be indispensable.

Yes, *the Catechism is a gift entrusted to us Bishops in particular.*

In you, venerable brothers, chairmen of the doctrinal commissions of the Episcopal Conferences throughout the world gathered here near the tomb of Peter, is expressed the joy of your brothers and the sons of the Church whom you represent: they are grateful to God that they can avail themselves of this instrument for the proclamation and witness of the faith.

At the same time, your participation in this solemn gathering expresses their firm desire to use this document in the varied ecclesial and cultural contexts which, as I have already noted on other occasions (cf. *Address to the Roman Curia* on June 28, 1986; *Discourse on the Approval of the Catechism,* June 25, 1992), must constitute the "point of reference", the *magna carta* for the prophetic message, and especially for catechetical proclamation, in particular through the preparation of local, national and diocesan catechisms, whose mediation should be considered indispensable.

May Mary help us accept and appreciate this gift

These sentiments and determination of yours were already expressed by your representative, Cardinal Bernard Francis Law, whom I cordially greet and thank.

11. Now, before concluding, I want to turn my thoughts with sentiments of filial love and due gratitude to her who accepted, meditated upon and gave the Word of the Father to humanity. On this solemn occasion, we recall the exhortation of the great Saint Ambrose: *"Sit in singulis Mariæ anima ut magnificet Dominum; sit in singulis Spiritus Mariæ ut exultet in Deo"* (St. Ambrose, *Exp. in Luc.,* II, 26; *PL* 15, 1642).

May the Blessed Virgin, whose Immaculate Conception we celebrate tomorrow, help us to accept and appreciate this precious gift and be a model and support for us in giving others the divine Word which the *Catechism of the Catholic Church* presents to the faithful and to the whole world.

VI

Catechism should serve new evangelization

Pope John Paul II
December 13, 1992
Third Sunday of Advent

Dear Brothers and Sisters,

1. While the echo created by the official presentation of the *Catechism of the Catholic Church* still resounds, I feel the need fervently to thank the Lord together with the whole Church, which on this occasion once again experienced the efficacious action of the Holy Spirit. The interest aroused by the new text, even beyond the limits of the Catholic communities, has shown itself to be of such proportions that it is difficult to attribute it to mere curiosity.

In this circumstance, which we could rightly call historic, the Church is happy to have had the opportunity to witness the great and wonderful "news" centered on the name of Jesus, Redeemer of mankind.

The Church feels *a lasting responsibility* for this "news" and its proclamation. Despite the burden of her frailty, with humble courage she assumes the task of making it resound before all humanity.

2. In this perspective, however, the promulgation of the new *Catechism* is not just an act of doctrinal regulation, but takes on the weight of an appeal addressed to all believers to *work with greater commitment in the new evangelization.*

We are now at the end of the 20th century, witnesses of a complex history, a frequently dramatic one, and its heritage will have a long-lasting effect. In whatever way history develops, this world of ours, however, with its lights and shadows, will continue to be the object of God's love and providence. It will be in ever greater need of love, hope, peace, of solidarity among peoples, of true justice for the oppressed, in the context of humanity's newfound equilibrium with nature and the cosmos.

3. Christianity contains the source and the "secret" of these realities, which constitute the perennial longing of the human heart, in the redemptive action of the incarnate Word; precisely during this season of Advent which prepares us for Christmas, the liturgy invites us to meditate and experience anew his first manifestation. Together with similar instruments of formation devised by the local Churches in every part of the world, the new *Catechism*, too, placed at the service of the Word of God, is meant to contribute to the joyous, ardent proclamation of that exhilarating "secret".

Dear brothers and sisters, may Mary accompany us in this new advent of the Christian proclamation. She who recognizes the time of God is calling the Church of our day to a renewed commitment of prayer and action on the threshold of the third Christian millennium.

With her we raise our prayer to the Spirit of God, the main agent of the new evangelization, so that the world may see the glory of the Saviour.

VII

Catechism is sure norm of doctrine

Letter of the Holy Father Pope John II
to Priests for Holy Thursday 1993
April 8, 1993

1. *"Jesus Christ is the same yesterday and today and forever"* (Heb 13: 8).

Dear Brothers in the priesthood of Christ!

As we gather today in the many different Cathedral Churches throughout the world—members of the presbyteral communities of all the Churches together with the Pastors of the Dioceses—there come back to our mind with new force these words about Jesus Christ which became the recurring theme of the 500th anniversary of the evangelization of the New World.

"Jesus Christ is the same yesterday and today and forever": these words refer to the *one eternal Priest,* who "entered once for all into the Holy Place, . . . with his own blood, thus securing an eternal redemption" (cf. Heb 9: 12). Now the days have come—the "Triduum Sacrum" of the Church's sacred liturgy—in which, with even deeper veneration and worship, we renew the Passover of Christ, "his hour" (cf. Jn 2: 4; 13: 1), which is the blessed "fullness of time" (cf. Gal 4: 4) . . .

Through the Eucharist, this "hour" of Christ's redemption contin-ues, in the Church, to be salvific. Today especially the Church recalls the institution of the Eucharist at the Last Supper. "I will not leave you desolate; I will come to you" (Jn 14: 18). The "hour" of the Redeemer, the "hour" of his going forth from this world to the

Father, the "hour" of which he himself says: "I go away, and I will come to you" (Jn 14: 28). Precisely through his "paschal going forth", Christ constantly comes to us and remains present among us, by the power of the Spirit, the Paraclete. He is present sacramentally. He is present through the Eucharist. He is really present.

Dear brothers, *after the Apostles we have received* this ineffable gift *so that we may be ministers of* Christ's *going forth* by way of the cross and, at the same time, *of* his *coming* in the Eucharist. How wonderful this Holy Triduum is for us! How wonderful for us is this day—the day of the Last Supper! We are ministers of the mystery of the redemption of the world, ministers of the Body which was offered and of the Blood which was shed so that sins might be forgiven. Ministers of that Sacrifice by which he, alone, entered once for all into the Holy Place. "Having offered himself without blemish to God, he purifies our conscience from dead works to serve the living God" (cf. Heb 9: 14).

Although all the days of our life are marked by this great mystery of faith, today is even more so. This is our day with him.

2. On this day we gather together in our *priestly communities,* so that each one can contemplate more deeply the mystery of the Sacrament whereby we have become ministers in the Church of Christ's priestly offering. We have likewise become servants of the royal priesthood of the whole People of God, of all the baptized, so that we may proclaim the *"magnalia Dei",* the "mighty works of God" (Acts 2: 11).

It is fitting to include in our thanksgiving this year *a particular element of gratitude* for the gift of the *Catechism of the Catholic Church.* This text is a response to the mission which the Lord has entrusted to his Church: to guard the deposit of faith and to hand it down intact, with authority and loving concern, to coming generations.

The result of the fruitful cooperation of the Bishops of the Catholic Church, the *Catechism* is entrusted above all to us, the Pastors of God's People, in order to strengthen our deep bonds of communion in the same apostolic faith. *As a compendium of the one perennial Catholic faith,* it constitutes a trustworthy and authoritative means for bearing witness to and ensuring that unity in faith for which Christ himself prayed fervently to the Father as his "hour" drew near (cf. Jn 17: 21-23).

The *Catechism* sets forth once more the fundamental and essential contents of Catholic faith and morality as they are believed, celebrated, lived and prayed by the Church today. It is thus *a special means* for deepening knowledge of the inexhaustible Christian mystery, for encouraging fresh enthusiasm for prayer intimately united with the prayer of Christ and for strengthening the commitment of a consistent witness of life.

At the same time, this *Catechism* is given to us as a *sure point of reference* for fulfilling the mission, entrusted to us in the Sacrament of Orders, of proclaiming the "Good News" to all people *in the name of Christ and of the Church.* Thanks to it, we can put into practice, in a constantly renewed way, Christ's perennial command: "Go therefore and make disciples of all nations . . . teaching them to observe all that I have commanded you" (Mt 28: 19-20).

Indeed, in this summary of the deposit of faith, we can find *an authentic and sure norm* for teaching Catholic doctrine, for catechetical activity among the Christian people, for that "new evangelization" of which today's world has such immense need.

Dear priests, our life and ministry will themselves become an eloquent catechesis for the entire community entrusted to us, provided that they are rooted in the Truth which is Christ. Then ours will not be an isolated witness, but a harmonious one, offered by people united in the same faith and sharing in the same cup. It is this sort of vital "infectiousness" that we must together aim at, in effective and affective communion, in order to carry out the ever more urgent "new evangelization."

3. Gathered on Holy Thursday in all the priestly communities of the Church throughout the world, we give thanks for the gift of Christ's priesthood which we share through the sacrament of Holy Orders. In this thanksgiving we wish to include the theme of the *Catechism,* because its contents and its usefulness are *particularly linked up with our priestly life and with the Church's pastoral ministry.*

In the journey towards the Great Jubilee of the Year 2000, the Church has succeeded in producing, after the Second Vatican Council, a compendium of her teaching on faith and morality, on sacramental life and prayer. This synthesis can support our priestly ministry in various ways. It can also enlighten the apostolic awareness of our brothers and sisters who, following their Christian vocation, desire together with us to account for that hope (cf. 1 Pt 3: 15) which gives us life in Jesus Christ.

The *Catechism* presents the *"newness of the Council"*, and at the same time situates it *in the whole of Tradition*. The *Catechism* is so filled with the treasures found in Sacred Scripture and in the Fathers and Doctors of the Church in the course of 2,000 years that it will enable each of us to become like the man in the Gospel parable "who brings out of his treasure what is new and what is old" (Mt 13 : 52), the ancient and ever new riches of the divine deposit.

Rekindling the grace of the Sacrament of Orders, conscious of what the *Catechism of the Catholic Church* means for our priestly ministry, we confess with worship and love the One who is "the way, and the truth, and the life" (Jn 14: 6).

"Jesus Christ is the same yesterday and today and forever."

From the Vatican, on April 8, Holy Thursday, in the year 1993, the 15th of my Pontificate.

Joannes Paulus pp. II

VIII

'Catechism of the Catholic Church' is a gift for all

Pope John Paul II
Thursday, April 29, 1993

In a special audience His Holiness addressed the Presidents of the Episcopal Conference Commissions for Catechesis and other participants in a workshop on preparing local catechisms.

Your Eminencies,
Dear Brothers in the Episcopate,
Dear Priests,
Brothers and Sisters,

1. With great pleasure I receive you on the occasion of the convention sponsored by the Congregation for the Clergy on a topic that is particularly timely and important for the life of the Church such as the *implications of the "Catechism of the Catholic Church" for the catechetical apostolate in general and for the preparation of local catechisms in particular.*

I thank Cardinal José T. Sánchez, Prefect of the Congregation, for the kind words he addressed to me, and with affection I greet the Presidents of the Episcopal Conference Commissions for Catechesis, as well as the experts and the members of the Congregation.

During this Easter season the words of St. Peter still resound in our hearts: the stone rejected by the builders "has become the cornerstone. There is no salvation through anyone else" (Acts 4: 11-12).

Jesus Christ is the eternal salvation which revealed itself in the fullness of time. He is the *truth* which sets free; the *word* which saves.

In order to communicate the Good News to all people, he founded his Church with the specific mission of evangelizing. After Pentecost, the Church enthusiastically obeyed her divine Founder's command, and began the mission of *spreading the Good News of salvation*.

This is what the Lord's disciples have done throughout human history. This is what the Church intends to do today, at the beginning of the third millennium, committed to achieving the *new evangelization, using for that purpose the "Catechism of the Catholic Church"*, a tool that fully responds to the demands of the present age.

Catechism presents complete message of Christ

2. The publication of that *Catechism* was hailed as a true gift of the Lord on the eve of the new millennium. In the world of today, marked by the worrisome processes of secularization frequently resulting in atheism, a world in which the heightened thirst for the sacred is frequently manifested in forms of subjectivism or in the multiplication of questionable religious movements, *there is widespread need for certainty in professing the faith and in the personal commitment to conversion* and Christian living.

The new *Catechism*, which by its very nature is a true and proper catechetical text, is meant to respond to this need; it will not fail to benefit the new evangelization, presenting the message of Christ in its entirety, without mutilation or falsification (cf. *Catechesi Tradendæ*, n. 30).

The new evangelization, whose success depends to a large extent on catechetical activity, has as its point of departure the certainty that in Christ there are "inscrutable riches" (cf. Eph 3: 8) which no culture and no era can exhaust and upon which people are continually called to draw in order to give direction to their life. *That wealth is first and foremost the person of Christ himself,* in whom we have access to the truth about God and man. Those who believe in him, no matter what era or culture they belong to, find the answer to the ever ancient but ever new questions concerning the mystery of existence that are indelibly imprinted on the human heart.

3. The new evangelization, however, requires first of all *a catechesis that, presenting the plan of salvation, "can call people to conversion"* and to hope in God's promise on the basis of certitude about the true resurrection of Christ, the first proclamation and root of all evangelization, the foundation of all human development and the principle of every genuinely Christian culture.

It is necessary for the Pastors of the People of God and pastoral workers to pay special attention to catechesis, which *is the systematic explanation of the first Gospel proclamation,* the education of those who are preparing to receive Baptism or ratify their commitment to it, the initiation into the Church's life and the concrete witness of charity. Catechesis is therefore a moment of essential importance in the rich and complex project of evangelization. As I also mentioned in the Letter which I recently addressed to all priests on the occasion of Holy Thursday, in the *Catechism* "we can find an authentic and sure norm . . . for catechetical activity among the Christian people, for that 'new evangelization' of which today's world has such immense need" (n. 2).

4. In the *Catechism of the Catholic Church* catechetical ministry finds *the most suitable instrument for the new evangelization.*

Church is Mother of our rebirth

It is urgent for each catechist, in virtue of his *charisma* and the mandate received from the Pastors, to repeat in the community the function of the *Church as Teacher,* the educator who, humble like her Lord, patiently leads every individual disciple to a plan of life of which she is not the author, but the trustee and mediator.

Never forgetting that it is God who teaches his people, and that it is Jesus Christ who is the interior teacher of his followers through the ceaseless gift of his Spirit, we do well to emphasize a principle which can inspire the pastoral use of the *Catechism of the Catholic Church,* and which we read in article 169 of the text itself:

"Salvation comes from God alone; however, because we receive the life of faith through the Church, she is our Mother: 'We believe *the Church,* as the Mother of our new birth, and not *in the Church,* as if she were the author of our salvation' (Faustus of Riez, *De Spiritu Sancto,* 1, 2). *Since she is our Mother, the Church is also our teacher in the faith.*"

5. The new *Catechism* is given to the Pastors and faithful because, like every genuine catechism, it serves to educate people in the faith which the Catholic Church professes and proclaims. However, it is a gift for all: *in fact, it is addressed to all and must reach everyone.* The extraordinary acclaim it has received from the Christian people serves the whole Church as a further reminder and encouragement in this important task.

Possessing a particular completeness of its own, this *Catechism* is also the *"type" and "exemplar" for other catechisms,* a sure reference text for teaching Catholic doctrine and in a very special way for drafting local catechisms. It *cannot be considered merely as a stage preceding the drafting of local catechisms,* but is destined for all the faithful who have the capacity to read, understand and assimilate it in their Christian living. In this perspective it becomes the support and foundation for the preparation of new catechetical tools which take the various cultural situations into consideration and together take pains to preserve the unity of the faith and fidelity to Catholic doctrine (cf. *Fidei Depositum,* n. 4).

6. The 1977 Synod of Bishops rightly affirmed that evangelization is *a dynamic initiative:* it is a question of incarnating the Gospel in cultures and accepting into Christianity the authentic values of the cultures themselves (cf. *Message to the People of God,* n. 5). This means that catechesis is committed to *preserving and passing on the entire depositum fidei* contained in the *Catechism of the Catholic Church* and to becoming an active factor in the inculturation of the faith.

In order to be a way leading to such inculturation, catechesis must make use of the *Catechism of the Catholic Church in the light of the fundamental truths of faith and the three great mysteries of salvation: Christmas,* which shows the way of the incarnation and leads the person who catechizes to *share his own life with those who are being catechized,* assuming all the positive elements possible such as their history, customs, tradition and culture, *Easter,* which through suffering leads to purification from sin and the *ransom of every culture* from the lack of sensitivity to evil and to the frailty of natural limitation; *Pentecost,* which, with the gift of the Holy Spirit, makes it possible for everyone to understand in his own language the mighty works of God, opening up new realms for the operation of faith and culture itself.

Incarnating the faith purifies cultures

7. It is clear that the Christian faith *is not identified with any given culture,* since it is above them, although it can be *de facto incarnated in the various cultures.* This means that every catechetical process must take into consideration and accept the divine initiative which gives the faith freely and fosters the human and cultural expression that transmits it. The Holy Spirit, who "fills the world, is all-embracing, and knows what man says" (Wis 1: 7), is the one who constantly gives the grace of every culture receiving and living the Gospel.

Incarnating the faith is not only an inevitable historical necessity, but also a necessary condition for the faith to be lived, deepened and communicated.

Such an action also necessarily has *a function of purification* in regard to cultures. It is precisely from the word of God that people are shown two paths: the paths of good and evil, inviting them to cast off the old man in order to be slaves of sin no longer (cf. Rom 6: 9-11) and to put on the new man created in the holiness of the truth. This presupposes a catechesis *capable of an in-depth understanding of the human condition* and, in the light of the kingdom of God, evangelically distinguishing the good fish from the bad (cf. Mt 13: 48).

In summary, the use of the *Catechism of the Catholic Church* in catechesis and local catechisms must be guided by this principle of communion: "compatibility with the Gospel and communion with the universal Church" *(Redemptoris Missio* n. 54).

May this principle, which has been at the basis of your work during these days, continue to guide you in the future too, helping you to succeed in a highly laudable enterprise, that of *offering to your faithful catechetical tools that are adapted to the needs of the times* and which achieve the new evangelization that is the challenge facing the whole Church at the end of this millennium.

In this essential and demanding task may you be accompanied and supported by my Blessing, which I affectionately impart to you, to your work, and to the Churches you represent and for which you generously devote your energy.

PART TWO

Reflections on the Catechism
of the Catholic Church

I

Catechism shows God's salvific will requires Church to be missionary

by Cardinal Jozef Tomko
Prefect of the Congregation for the Evangelization of Peoples

At the time of the solemn presentation of the *Catechism of the Catholic Church* I was on a pastoral visit in the missionary territories of that vast "submerged continent" of Oceania. The news had already reached even the islands scattered throughout the vast expanse of the Pacific waters and a number of educated lay persons approached me to tell me how impatient they were for the book's arrival, because it would provide them with a means of nourishing their faith. It was an indication of the enthusiasm for this "faith-generating text" to be found even in the most remote corners of the world.

This little episode confirms the catechism's importance for mission countries. However, the work is also of great importance for the entire world, because, as the Holy Father said, "the new *Catechism* will give the faithful an invaluable opportunity to rekindle their faith and strengthen their missionary spirit, thus fostering an authentic renewal of the Church."

Mission permeates *Catechism*

In fact, the missionary dimension is, as it were, the spirit permeating the entire book. I am speaking of the *Catechism* which the Catholic Church gives us in anticipation of the great Jubilee of the year 2000, as the Spirit is guiding the Churches on all continents toward evangelization (or toward the new evangelization), which is the theme of this year's regional meetings: of the Synods for Europe and for Africa, of the plenary meeting of the Bishops of Asia in 1991 and of the recent conference of Latin-American Bishops at Santo Domingo. The Catholic Church, which at the Second Vatican Council defined herself as missionary by nature *(Ad Gentes,* n. 2), is now presented in the *Catechism* as "communion and mission." For this reason in the *Catechism* the missionary aspect is sometimes explicit, sometimes implicit, but always an essential characteristic. One need only glance at its thematic index to see the wealth of references to terms such as "mission", "mission *Ad Gentes",* "missionary", "evangelization", "salvation", "proclamation", etc.

Certainly, the new *Catechism* is not a missiology handbook. Nevertheless, the missionary spirit can be found even in the sections treating the mysteries of the faith, in the celebration of the Christian mystery in the Sacraments, in the section on morality, and in the section on prayer. Nor could it be otherwise if one recalls that mission has its ultimate source in the "mission *ad intra"* within the Blessed Trinity that extends from within the intimate life of God into the mission of the Son in virtue of the Holy Spirit and continues in the mission entrusted to the Church and to every baptized person: "Go and make disciples of all nations" (Mt 28: 19); "you are to be my witnesses even to the ends of the earth" (Acts 1: 8), witnesses by your lives and by means of the word, nourished by the sacraments and by prayer.

However, in some chapters the missionary dimension is more explicit. There is a brief but incisive part in which the idea of mission is treated directly, *ex professo,* as it were, in the context of the Church's catholicity.

'Mission: a demand of the Church's catholicity'

Concisely and succinctly, sometimes in a manner reminiscent of the solemn professions of faith, the *Catechism* outlines the basis of mission. These well-honed truths are taken from Scripture and the documents of the Second Vatican Council, and supplemented by the missionary Encyclical of John Paul II, *Redemptoris Missio,* which in the *Catechism* finds its just and ever more widely acknowledged doctrinal application. In the certitudes drawn from the sources of faith one finds an implicit response to some theological opinions which today still threaten not only missionary activity, but also the Church's catholicity and missionary identity.

The foundation of mission is indicated in the Lord's *missionary mandate* (Mt 28: 19-20): "Sent by God to the nations in order to be a 'universal Sacrament of salvation', the Church, in virtue of the most profound requirements of her catholicity and in obedience to the command of her Founder, strives to announce the Gospel to all people" *(Catechism,* n. 849; *Ad Gentes,* n. 7). This is a decisive response to those who would like to reduce the missionary effort to the era of colonialism and to proclaim its demise.

Having shown that *the origin* of mission is in the eternal love of the Blessed Trinity and that its *goal* is to make all human beings sharers of the fellowship that exists among the Persons of the Trinity (cf. *Redemptoris Missio,* n. 23), the *Catechism* describes the *reason* for mission as follows:

"The Church has always derived the obligation and the strength of her missionary drive from the *love* of God for all human beings: 'the love of Christ impels us . . .' (2 Cor 5: 14). 'For God wants all men to be saved and come to know the truth' (1 Tm 2: 4). God wills the salvation of all through the knowledge of the truth. Salvation is found in the truth. Those who are obedient to the movement of the Spirit of truth are already on the road to salvation; but the Church, to whom this truth has been entrusted, must respond to their desire, by offering it to them. Precisely because she believes in the universal plan of salvation, the Church must be missionary" *(Catechism,* n. 851).

This rich passage clarifies many questions under discussion in the missionary world today. Above all, it specifies that God's universal salvific will includes the knowledge of the saving truth, as is clear from the Pauline text which is sometimes truncated in biased citations. From this it follows that the universal divine plan to save all people not only does not prevent or diminish the

Church's missionary outreach to non-Christians, but rather supplies it with an even greater encouragement and stimulus.

New emphases are likewise found in the section on the *paths of mission,* which include the way of the cross, of poverty and of patience, and admit various forms and phases of evangelization: proclamation, establishment of the Christian community and foundation of the local Churches, inculturation, the purpose of which is to incarnate the Gospel in local cultures; respectful dialogue with those who do not yet accept the Gospel.

Mission and the salvation of non Christians

In the context of the Church's catholicity, the *Catechism* also addresses her relationship to non-Christian religions, a question which has a direct bearing on mission and which is increasingly debated today. Here, too, we find a synthesis of patristic and conciliar doctrine which succeeds in condensing into two pages the principles which can shed light on the problems that increased contact with these religions has made an ever greater focus of concern for theologians and Christians in general. Obviously, for a missionary Church the catechism's responses on this matter are of fundamental importance, although the topic can be found throughout the teaching of the Second Vatican Council.

First of all, with the Council the *Catechism* affirms that "'those who have not yet received the Gospel are related to the People of God in various ways" *(Lumen Gentium,* n. 16). Then it gives special consideration to the Church's relationship with the Jewish people and with Muslims. Passing then to other non-Christian religions, it points to the Church's bond with them above all in terms of the common origin and common end of the human race (cf. *Nostra Ætate,* n. 1).

In extremely concise but also carefully balanced language, the *Catechism* then describes the situation of these religions (nn. 843-845):

"'The Church recognizes in other religions the search, still in shadows and images', for 'an Unknown God' but one who is near, 'because it is he who gives life and breath to all, and . . . wills that all men be saved'. For this reason 'whatever good or truth' is found in religions the Church considers to be 'a preparation for the Gospel', given by him who enlightens all men that they may at length have life" *(Lumen Gentium,* n. 16; *cf. Nostra Ætate,* n. 2, *Evangelii Nuntiandi,* n. 53).

"But in their religious behavior people also reveal the limitations and errors which mar God's image that is in them." "But very often, deceived by the Evil One, people have become vain in their reasonings, have exchanged the truth of God for a lie and served the world rather than the Creator. Or else, living and dying in this world without God, they are exposed to ultimate despair" *(Lumen Gentium,* n. 16).

"Precisely in order to reunite once again all his children, scattered and led astray by sin, the Father has willed to summon all humanity into the Church of his Son. The Church is the place in which humanity must find unity and salvation."

At this point the *Catechism* touches on the question of the necessity of the Church for salvation. It explains above all the true sense of the adage *"extra Ecclesiam nulla salus*—outside the Church there is no salvation"; it means simply that all salvation comes from Christ the Head through the Church which is his Body (cf. *Lumen Gentium,* n. 14). It then continues in the words of the Second Vatican Council, clarifying the situation of those who, through no fault of their own, are ignorant of Christ and of the Church:

"Those who, through no fault of their own, do not know the Gospel of Christ or his Church, but who nevertheless seek God with a sincere heart, and, moved by grace, try in their actions to do his will as they know it through the dictates of their conscience—those too may achieve eternal salvation" *(Lumen Gentium,* n. 16).

And it concludes: "Although in ways known to himself God can lead those who, through no fault of their own, are ignorant of the Gospel to that faith without which it is impossible to please him, the Church, nevertheless, still has the obligation and also the sacred right to evangelize (*Ad Gentes,* n. 7) all people."

A sure guide for mission

There are many other relevant questions in mission territories for which the *Catechism* gives a clear and firm direction. Let it suffice to mention, for example, the teaching on marriage in reference to polygamy and divorce, or that of the matter to be used in the sacraments, the teaching on salvation in Jesus Christ, the one Mediator, etc.

In general one could say that for mission lands the *Catechism* has a special role as a sure guide for sustaining and confirming the faith and for pursuing evangelization with doctrinal certitude.

The young Churches, their pastors and missionaries will find in the *Catechism* a clear point of reference not only for proclaiming the true faith but above all for the delicate task of inculturating the Gospel and incarnating it in the local cultures—a task which requires a perfect knowledge of the content of faith in order to be able to compare it with the contents of a culture and to evaluate their compatibility with the Gospel and with the spirit of communion with the universal Church (cf. *Familiaris Consortio*, n. 10).

The *Catechism* will be of invaluable assistance for these young Churches, enabling them to establish a link with the Church's millennia of Tradition and at the same time with the period of postconciliar renewal, thus receiving the *nova et vetera*, new things and old, of the life of faith, without unnecessary risks and hitches.

For the entire Church it will be "a valid and legitimate instrument for ecclesial communion and a sure norm for teaching the faith", as the Holy Father states in the Apostolic Constitution *Fidei Depositum* which accompanied the publication of the *Catechism*. With its pronounced missionary dimension it will lead the universal Church and the particular Churches, especially those with a missionary stamp, to a new evangelization effort.

The wish expressed by Pope John Paul II in the same Constitution that serves as an introduction to the *Catechism* takes on special depth when it is read in a missionary perspective: "May the light of the true faith free humanity from ignorance and slavery to sin in order to lead it to the only freedom worthy of the name (cf. Jn 8: 32): that of life in Jesus Christ under the guidance of the Holy Spirit."

II

Catechism's origin and content reflect Episcopal collegiality

by Archbishop Jan P. Schotte
Secretary General Synod of Bishops

During the official presentation of the *Catechism of the Catholic Church,* which took place in the *Sala Regia* of the Apostolic Palace in the Vatican at noon on December 7, 1992, the Holy Father gave a speech in which, among other things, he made the following statement: "The *Catechism of the Catholic Church* is a qualified, authoritative instrument which the Church's Pastors desired first of all for themselves, as a valuable help in fulfilling the mission they have received from Christ to proclaim and witness the Good News to all people."

On the following day, December 8, in his homily at Saint Mary Major, he called that document "the postconciliar *Catechism*", because it "is a compendium of the truth proclaimed by the Church throughout the world." And he added: "This compendium of the Catholic faith, requested by the Bishops gathered in the Extraordinary Assembly of the Synod in 1985, is the most mature and complete fruit of the Council's teaching and presents it in the rich framework of the whole of ecclesial Tradition."

From the Council through the Synod

The words of the Holy Father offer ample room for reflection on and investigation of that truth marvelously professed by the Second Vatican Council: the collegiality of the Bishops whose unity is presided over by the Bishop of Rome in the communion of the primatial pastoral mandate. *Cum Petro et sub Petro.*

The Council's teaching is rich in this area and has enjoyed continuous success in the postconciliar era in an exercise which has reached the particular Churches, the Episcopal Conferences and their various organisms of communion and pastoral praxis.

The most immediately evident form of collegiality after the Council seems to be the Synod of Bishops itself, in which that communion is made present and is exercised in an affective and effective way. In an address to the Council of the General Secretariat of the Synod of Bishops on April 30, 1983, Pope John Paul II said: "The Synod is in fact a particularly fruitful expression and the most effective tool of episcopal collegiality, that is, of the special responsibility of the Bishops in conjunction with the Bishop of Rome."

From the historical viewpoint it becomes clear from an examination of the various acts of the Synod that all the meetings have directed their efforts to a practical development of conciliar doctrine, thus showing a direct continuity with the Second Vatican Council, which, like every Council, represents the primary act of collegiality.

It is historical fact that the *Catechism of the Catholic Church* was conceived in Synod.

The Fourth Ordinary General Assembly of the Synod of Bishops, which was held in 1977, gave ample treatment to the question of catechesis and its renewal. Its *Lineamenta* speak generally of the necessity of a clear presentation of doctrine. Its *Instrumentum laboris* referred to the updating of catechisms and of audio-visual aids in the teaching of the doctrine of the faith. The *relatio ante disceptationem* raised specific questions about the need to prepare a "basic catechism". The Apostolic Exhortation published after that Synod, *Catechesi Tradendœ,* makes further mention of drafting a "genuine catechism".

At the Extraordinary Assembly of 1985 four Bishops made a concrete proposal for a catechism at the level of the universal Church during the *disceptatio* at the beginning of the Synod. This idea was then examined in greater depth in the small groups and illustrated at some length in the reports of six of the 12 language groups and included in the *Relatio finalis* which was put to a vote. This proposal to "draft a catechism or compendium of all of Catholic doctrine regarding faith and morals" was voted almost unanimously—155 votes, with 146 (94%) in favor.

The proposal of the catechism stemmed from this almost unanimous consensus of the Pastors in communion with Peter, an idea which the Holy Father fully accepted when he established the special Pontifical Commission for the *Catechism* of the Universal Church.

Other historical data show that the creation of the catechism was the product of a profound spirit of effective episcopal collegiality.

For the literary composition of the document, 12 Cardinals and Bishops representing all the continents were called by the Holy Father to serve on the Commission; they in turn were assisted, in the executive phase, by an editorial committee composed of seven diocesan Bishops, representatives of the major cultural contexts, assisted by many experts in the various branches of theology who were likewise drawn from the many geographical and linguistic areas, and also from the Secretariat formed within the Congregation for the Doctrine of the Faith.

The Episcopate of the whole Church was called to collaborate through a formal consultation process that was to assure the final product's seriousness and credibility. In fact, the draft text was submitted to the Bishops for their study, suggestions and observations.

In presenting the text to the Holy Father, Cardinal Ratzinger, Prefect of the above-mentioned Congregation and President of the Commission for the *Catechism*, said: "The *Catechism of the Catholic Church* is the result of a collegial episcopal effort." The statement is undeniable and its positive significance is confirmed by the fact that collegiality was singled out as the primary characteristic in the preparation of the *Catechism* itself.

The Cardinal continued: "Desired by a Synod of Bishops, drawn up by diocesan Bishops, in one of the stages of its composition it was examined by the entire Catholic Episcopates . . .. Thus, once again, the affective and effective collegiality of the Episcopate has been engaged in real and concrete terms, with abundantly fruitful results."

Doctrine of collegiality

The practice of collegiality manifested in the catechism's formative stages finds significant confirmation in its doctrinal exposition.

Various references scattered throughout the work provide the essential elements for a correct and complete definition of episcopal collegiality.

Collegiality is in the first instance "apostolic". Indeed "in the college of the Twelve, Simon Peter occupies the first place" (n. 552). The ministry entrusted to Peter comes to light precisely in the place where it originates and to which it relates in a fundamental way, that is, the college of the Apostles. "The power to 'bind and loose' . . . was conferred by Jesus on the Church through the ministry of the Apostles and particularly of Peter, the only one to whom the keys of the kingdom were explicitly entrusted" (*ibid.* and n. 1444).

"The college of Bishops, with whom the priests are united in the priesthood, makes present and actualizes the college of the Twelve until Christ returns" (n. 1577)

"The Church is apostolic, because she is founded on the Apostles . . .. Until Christ's return, she continues to be instructed, sanctified and guided by the Apostles through their successors in the pastoral mission: the college of Bishops, with the assistance of the priests and in union with the Successor of Peter, the supreme Pastor of the Church" (n. 857).

Collegiality can also be called "sacramental", in the sense that entrance into this "apostolic" collegiality takes place through episcopal consecration.

"The collegial character and nature of the episcopal order is revealed, among other things, in the Church's ancient practice requiring the participation of a number of Bishops for the consecration of a new Bishop. For the legitimate ordination of a Bishop, a special intervention of the Bishop of Rome is required today because he is the supreme visible bond of the communion of the particular Churches in the one Church and the guarantor of their freedom. As vicar of Christ, every Bishop has the pastoral office of the particular Church which has been entrusted to him, but at the same time he bears a concern for all the Churches in collegiality with all his brothers" (nn. 1559 and 1560).

Thus, all the proper elements of collegiality are spelled out in the catechism's statements:

- its origin in the will of the Lord;
- its link with the college of the Apostles;
- its necessary relationship to the primacy of Peter;
- the pastoral ministry of collegial service;
- the collegial responsibility of the Bishops for the universal Church;
- the sacramental aspect of entrance into the episcopal college;
- its connatural relation to priestly orders;
- the eschatological dynamism of the collegial mission.

Collegiality and 'tradition'

The *Catechism of the Catholic Church* is a tool for the profession and transmission of the faith. We might ask ourselves: to whom is it entrusted?

The answer to this question contains a nucleus which presupposes and sheds light on the doctrine and praxis of the collegiality of the Bishops in communion with the Pope.

The *de facto* collegiality manifested in the catechism's origin will be followed by the collegial commitment to ensuring its success.

Referring to the *Catechism* in the address cited above, the Holy Father says that "it is a qualified, authoritative instrument which the Church's Pastors desired first of all for themselves."

Thus that instrument, born of the collegiality of the Bishops, is destined, is entrusted, to those same Bishops.

In the Church the act of entrusting does not consist in a mere handing on from one person to the next. In the Church *tradere* is a crucial word.

In the liturgy of the sacraments, for example, there is a *traditio instrumentorum*, which indicates the handing over of material objects indispensable for the exercise of the powers received in the sacrament itself.

Similar to this physical act, but not extraneous to it, the true and proper *traditio fidei* is perpetuated in the community of believers through the action of the Spirit of the Lord, as testimony to the faith that has been received and handed on.

Within the current of this *traditio*, or, in the words of the Holy Father, "within the rich framework of the whole of ecclesial Tradition", there is, and not merely by way of an external act, the entrusting of a book, which is, like the *Catechism*, a book of the faith and for the faith, a particular *instrumentum fidei*.

In fact, this volume deserves the title *documentum fidei,* because it is born of the faith, expresses it, nourishes it and teaches it.

If the Bishops are *apostolicæ fidei magistri*, it would seem sufficiently natural that they should have in collegiality felt the pastoral responsibility to compose the book, "the postconciliar *Catechism*", a collegial work, and above all, to intend it for themselves, as the Pope said.

The fact that they entrusted it to themselves should not cause people to think we are dealing with a kind of sterile closed circuit, without any missionary outreach.

In fact, a clear distinction should be made between the catechism's destination and its goal. The words of the Pope are clear: its objective is to become "a valuable help in the fulfilling of the mission." Thus one could say that it is entrusted to the Bishops for the good of the Church!

Such acts of the Bishops' collegial, pastoral self-awareness are not very frequent, but when they do occur, as in the present case, they take on a special character.

Conclusion

As successors of the Apostles, the Bishops are given the mission to teach by word and with their lives.

Throughout the centuries the history of the catechism reflects the ministry of the proclamation and witness desired by the Lord.

The necessary relationship with the Lord, who entrusts and renders fruitful this mandate and service, shows that in the Church there is really only one Master: Christ. For this reason, he has promised us his Spirit of truth, who leads us into the whole truth.

The composition of the *Catechism of the Catholic Church* has been, as it were, historical proof of the relevance of this promise in the last few years of the second millennium and in the future we face.

The Spirit of truth, as we have been authoritatively reminded, has guided the work that went into the composition of the text: in truth and unity within the great ecclesial communion, the *Plures* of the college, the direct reference and the high place of collegiality, were gathered around the *unus Magister,* whom they confessed, celebrated and proclaimed together to the whole Church which prays: *"Pater noster, . . . adveniat regnum tuum."*

III

The divine economy interwoven through new catechetical work

by Christoph Schönborn, O. P.
Auxiliary Bishop of Viena, Austria

I am limiting my discussion to describing a few technical aspects of the plan of the new *Catechism of the Catholic Church* (Editorial aspects) and I shall then pinpoint some of the great theological topics that mark this work (The *'nexus mysteriorum'* in the new *Catechism*).

Editorial aspects

Originally, this *Catechism* was designed to be in three parts. It was then expanded to include a fourth part, following the example of the *Roman Catechism*. The editors of the critical edition of the latter, Pedro Rodriguez and Raúl Lanzetti[1], have provided some valuable information as to the meaning of the selection made by the editors of the *Catechism* of Trent. They call attention to the fact that the order of the four parts is of great theological significance.

The sequence of creed-sacraments-commandments-Our Father is not immediately apparent. St. Thomas had explained the Apostles' Creed, the Ten Commandments and the Our Father in a very simple catechesis preached in the Neapolitan dialect. For years these three texts have been the pillars of the Christian catechism,[2] and the Protestant tradition has preserved them.

The place that the Tridentine catechism gives to the sacraments is surprising. They would rightly have their place in the text of the creed under the "*Communio sanctorum*" section, and it was here that the German Bishops' catechism placed them. According to the editors of the Tridentine catechism, there were two more immediate reasons for another choice: the urgency of the doctrine of the sacraments in the 16th-century context, and linked to this reason, the enormous size which the text of the *Communio sanctorum* would otherwise have become. But there is still another more theological reason.

The proportion of each of the four parts of the Tridentine catechism is significant: 22% deals with the creed, 37% the sacraments (almost twice as much!) 21% and 20% the commandments and the Lord's Prayer, respectively.

Thus there is a clear "imbalance" in favor of the sacraments. A quick glance at the *Catechism of the Catholic Church* shows a different emphasis: 39% deals with the creed, 23% with the sacraments, 27% the commandments and 11% with prayer.

If in both cases there are historical circumstances partially influencing the divisions, the circumstances in which they were drafted or concerning the various stages of the text's development, there is also a theological and catechetical message, whether or not it was intended by the editors. In both texts, the Tridentine catechism and the *Catechism of the Catholic Church,* the first two parts together form about 60% of the text, that is, almost two thirds. Interpreting this fact, we can apply to the new *Catechism* what the editors said of the Tridentine text:

"Indeed, the order of the doctrine of the Tridentine catechism does not have four parts; it is presented to us as a magnificent diptych, in line with Tradition: here, the mysteries of faith in the one and triune God professed (creed) and celebrated (sacraments); there, human existence according to the faith—faith working through charity—is expressed through a rule of Christian life (Decalogue) and filial prayer (Our Father)."[3]

The message of this "diptych" is clear: in the catechetical explanation of the faith, whatever the method and the division of the contents, the primacy belongs to God and his works. Whatever human beings do will always be a response to the work of God. In the catechisms, the *magnalia Dei* are the important element in the text. This is a very clear cut theocentric emphasis.

Its explanation is not only doctrinal, it is doxological, it is confession and profession of the *facta et dicta* of God for our benefit, through pure grace.

There is yet another consideration that highlights the primacy of grace. The editors of the Tridentine catechism have pointed it out. Why in the Tridentine catechism are faith and the sacraments of faith put together, before the text of the Decalogue? The answer to this question is at the same time an answer to the objection made many times to the new catechism's structure. Why use the Ten Commandments in treating morals? Is this not "slipping back" into the Old Testament? Should it not have followed the Beatitudes or the theological virtues?

The authors of the Tridentine catechism are familiar with the concept of justification as it was explained by the Council of Trent, which determined their choice in the matter. Justification is linked to the sacraments of Baptism and Penance, which make human beings new creatures by giving them "the gifts of the Holy Spirit" and, therefore, grace and virtues.

Here I would like to quote several lines of the beautiful passage that the editors of the Tridentine catechism devoted to this view of their work, the inspiration for which was still alive during the drafting of the new *Catechism*:

"The choice is obvious: before telling Christians what they must do, we encounter this expression of St. Leo the Great: 'Recognize, O Christian, your dignity'. It is when Christ's faithful recognize the supernatural power that comes from their being in Christ through the Holy Spirit that they can commit themselves confidently, without servile fear, to the exercise and growth of their Christian existence as proposed by the Decalogue.

"Without being preceded by the doctrine of the sacraments which also includes the teaching on the Church and on justification, the precepts of the Decalogue would seem to surpass human strength. However, backed by faith and the sacraments, one can consider them with full trust and strength."[4]

"Now despite its Roman authority, (the) creed-sacraments-commandments sequence (of the catechism of Trent) would not be preserved in Catholic catechesis."[5] The creed-commandments-sacraments plan was to be far more frequent. Of course, this plan could draw inspiration from St. Augustine's *De catechizandis rudibus*. St. Peter Canisius's authority confirmed this, but it was not without danger. "This plan, in which the Decalogue follows the creed and precedes the sacraments, reflects less a specific tendency than the general 18th-century tendency to moralism. The Second Part will grow out of proportion through exhortations and moral precepts, even though the parts devoted to the creed and the sacraments are reduced." Will the new *Catechism* share the fate of the Tridentine catechism, "admired but not imitated?"

The *'nexus mysteriorum'* in the new *Catechism*

When in 1989 the "revised draft" of the *Catechism of the Catholic Church* was submitted for consultation to the whole Catholic Episcopate, one of the main criticisms expressed by a whole group of North American theologians was that this project did not respect the principle of the hierarchy of truths.[6] On examining the criticisms and suggestions of the Bishops and their experts, the Catechism Commission was particularly concerned about this issue of the hierarchy of truths.

In his report to the Synod of Bishops on 27 October 1990, Cardinal Ratzinger, President of the Commission, summarized its reply. The catechism's very outline was an expression of the hierarchy of truths: the four pillars of catechesis already articulate it in a systematic way, because what matters regarding the hierarchy of truths is the organic unity of the exposition and not, as some critics appear to think, the various degrees of certainty.

It is indeed necessary to distinguish clearly between the hierarchy of truths and the degrees of certainty. The *Catechism* must certainly avoid giving the impression that all the statements it contains have the same degree of certainty. It would be neither practical nor desirable constantly to indicate these degrees (*de fide, de fide definita, sententia communis*, etc.). Rather, the doctrine's degree of certainty should be evident from the context, from the way it is stated, from the doctrinal authority of the statement.

More important for catechesis is the principle of the organic unity of the exposition. Has the new *Catechism* succeeded in satisfying this need? It will be up to its readers to judge. I should simply like to present some guidelines as to how the text has been arranged.

Is there a *leitmotiv* running through the whole of the new *Catechism?* There was no explicit effort to provide one; however, it is certain that the theme of the *divine economy* is woven through all four parts.

Thus the First Part begins by explaining all the economy of Revelation, which culminates in the mystery of Christ. The Trinitarian structure of the Apostles' Creed is the expression of the Trinitarian character of the divine economy. In the first article of the creed ("I believe in God the Father") the new *Catechism* professes right from the start the truths concerning the very life of God in his Trinitarian mystery (nn. 232 ff.).

The whole of the divine economy has no other source or purpose than this infinitely blissful life: the economy is therefore expressed in accordance with the great moments of the communication of this life: the work of creation and divine governance (Providence), the work of redemption through Jesus Christ and the work of sanctification in the Holy Spirit through the Church.

The Second Part explicitly extends this perspective of the economy: in the age of the Church it becomes a sacramental economy. Therefore liturgical life in its entirety appears in the form of the "dispensation of the Mystery": the signs and the seasons, the sacraments and the sacramentals.

The theme of the economy is less evident in the Third Part. It appears above all in the articles on law and grace that more specifically address the divine dispositions to help us live according to God. It is very much present in the fourth part.

If the divine economy is a sort of *leitmotiv* running through the new *Catechism,* this economy itself gravitates around a centre, i.e., *the mystery of the Trinity*.

This is what the new *Catechism* says: "The mystery of the Blessed Trinity is the central mystery of faith and Christian life. It is the mystery of God in himself. Thus it is the source of all the other mysteries of faith, the light that illumines them. It is the most basic and essential teaching of the 'hierarchy of truths' of the faith (*General Catechetical Directory*, n. 43)" (n. 234).

And the new *Catechism* quotes the *General Catechetical Directory*, n. 47: "The whole history of salvation is none other than the history of the way and the means through which the true and only God, Father, Son and Holy Spirit, reveals himself, is reconciled and united to human beings who turn away from sin."

To be faithful to the "hierarchy of truths" is thus first of all to pay attention to the Trinitarian form of the exposition. The editors have tried to show clearly the links between the truths of faith and their Trinitarian basis. They have highlighted in particular the texts on creation, the Church, liturgy and prayer.

Purpose of catechesis is union with Christ

With the Trinitarian mystery there is a second basis to which the other truths of faith must refer in their hierarchy: *the mystery of Christ*. It can be said that this *Catechism* is profoundly Trinitarian, and it can equally and just as truly be said that it is *Christocentric*.

"At the heart of catechesis we find, in essence, a person, the person of Jesus of Nazareth, the only Son from the Father." "In catechesis it is Christ, the incarnate Word and Son of God, who is taught—everything else is taught with reference to him." These well known words of *Catechesi Tradendæ* (nn. 5-6) show clearly how the principle of the hierarchy of truths should be applied: everything should be referred to the basis that is Christ, because, *Catechesi Tradendæ* (n. 5) states further: "Only he can lead us to the love of the Father in the Spirit and make us share in the life of the Holy Trinity."

The purpose of teaching about Christ is to establish communion with him. The whole Christology of the new *Catechism* is marked by our communion in the mystery of Christ. His conception and birth, his hidden life and public ministry, his passion and resurrection are all shown in the perspective of the "mysteries of the life of Christ." Overcoming the perspective of mere imitation of Christ, the "mysteries of the life of Christ" are offered to us as an invitation to a communion of life.

This is a key text of the new *Catechism* (n. 521), which in turn refers to a key text of Vatican II, very often quoted by Pope John Paul II: "Everything that Christ experienced, we must be able to experience in us. 'By his incarnation, he, the Son of God, has in a certain way united himself with each person' *(Gaudium et Spes,* n. 22, 2) . . . What he lived in his flesh for us and as our model, he communicated to us as members of his body."

It is in the perspective of communion of life under the theme of "the members of his body" that the sacraments are presented. Two passages, one from Scripture and the other from the patristic tradition, clearly indicate this viewpoint.

Number 1116 states: "The sacraments as strength that springs from the Body of Christ (cf. Lk 5: 17, 6: 19, 8: 46), ever alive and enlivening, and as actions of the Holy Spirit at work in his Body, that is the Church: are 'God's masterpieces' of the new and eternal Covenant."

And in n. 1115 we read: "The mysteries of Christ's life are the foundations of what henceforth, through the ministers of his Church, Christ dispenses in the sacraments, because 'what was visible in our Lord has passed into his mysteries' (St. Leo the Great, *Sermon 74,* n. 2)."

The sacraments of Christ prolong the mysteries of his life and make us share in it. They are the forces that come from his Body, the Church. Thus it is not surprising that the text about the Church runs along the same lines. The ecclesiological explanation encourages a sacramental view of the Church, which is precisely the basis of Chapter 1 of *Lumen Gentium:* a Trinitarian view of the Church, the People of God, the Body of Christ and Temple of the Holy Spirit; a divine-human view of the Church based on an analogy with the incarnate Word (cf. *Lumen Gentium,* n. 8).

In this *Catechism* the faith and the sacraments are presented in their organic structure based on a twofold foundation: Trinitarian and Christological.

The "Revised Draft" of 1989 has been blamed for making too great a separation between faith and life by treating them in two different parts, the first and the third. I hope I have shown that another intention led to the choice of the plan: that of making it understood that Christian life is born as a person's free response to God's gifts and call, a response made possible by faith and the sacraments of faith.

The First Section of Part III, "fundamental morality", is built on the perspective of human action and God's action. The starting point is therefore man's call to holiness, as the First Part was begun with the theme of the quest for happiness. It goes on to explain the elements of man's free action: freedom itself, without which there is no responsibility, and therefore no good or bad actions; conscience, the judgment of reason regarding our acts; the human virtues generated by repeated good actions and the theological virtues, infused by God; finally, wrong actions, sin. The communal perspective of human action is then developed in the light of *Gaudium et Spes* and other pontifical documents.

Emphasis put on moral virtues

Nevertheless, without the help of the divine law that instructs and divine grace that elevates, the human person would not be able to respond adequately to God's call. It is evident that on the level of "fundamental morality", in addition to *Gaudium et Spes*, inspiration comes above all from the *Summa Theologiæ* of St. Thomas Aquinas. This is a clearly conscious choice. In a remarkable way this allows for an organic exposition of human freedom and divine grace; hence "synergy", cooperation alone can lead to the goal to which all human beings are called: holiness (cf. nn. 2012-2016).

The view of the human and theological virtues also characterizes the text on the Ten Commandments. For each commandment, the explanation does not begin with prohibitions, but with their corresponding virtues: thus, for the first commandment, the theological virtue is the virtue of religion, for the fourth, filial piety, for the sixth, chastity, for the seventh justice, for the eighth veracity.

It cannot be said that the Commission's decision to maintain the Ten Commandments as the framework of moral catechesis has ultimately been to the detriment of the virtues. One can see, for example, on reading the articles on the ninth and tenth commandments, how the Decalogue leads to the Beatitudes, principally the first, that of the poor in spirit to whom the kingdom of heaven is promised. This is certainly the perspective of the fourth part. Although it recognizes the "universal call to prayer" (n. 2566), to which the innate desire for prayer corresponds, the explanation of prayer is permeated with the spirit of the Beatitudes.

I would like to conclude these considerations of the overall structure and criteria used in drafting the new *Catechism* by calling attention to a new fact. One could say many things about the *nova et vetera* of this *Catechism*, which is at the same time very traditional and very new.

One point, I feel, deserves particular attention. What is unusual for this kind of document are the *many references to the testimony of saintly men and women*. The saints alone are sufficiently universal, Catholic, to speak to everyone in words that are born of the life and truth of faith. How could one doubt that the words of a St. Catherine, a St. Theresa of Avila or the "Little Flower" will have the power to cross all cultural and human boundaries to tell everyone, in a language impassioned by the love of Christ, the ancient and ever new truths of the Good News of Christ?

Notes

1   *Catechismus Romanus,* ed. P. Rodríguez *et al.,* Città Del Vaticano-Pamplona, 1989.

2   In his *Compendium* St. Thomas linked these three pillars with the three theological virtues: "Three things are necessary to be saved: to know what one must believe; to know what one must desire and to know what one must do. The first we are taught by the creed in which the knowledge of the articles of faith is transmitted; the second by the Lord's Prayer, the third in the law" *(Introduction to Opusculum III; In duo prœcepta caritatis et in Decem legis Prœcepta Expositio;* critical edition by J. P. Torrell in *RS Ph Th 69 (1985), p. 24.*

3   Op. cit., p. XXVIII.

4   Op. cit., p. XXVI-XXVIII; cf. Fr. Rodríguez, "El sentido de los Sacramentos según el *Catecismo Romano*", in *Scripta Theológica 9* (1977), 951-984.

5   J.-R. Armogathe, "De la loi à l'Amour", in *Communio* XVII, 1, (1992), p. 5.

6   *The Universal Catechism Reader: Reflections and Responses,* ed. Thomas J. Rease, S.J., San Francisco 1990.

IV

Eastern tradition reflected in new catechism's spirituality

by Guy-Paul Noujeim
Maronite Patriarchal Vicar
of Sarba-Kesrouan, Lebanon

"Father, . . . this is eternal life, that they should know you, the only true God, and the one whom you sent, Jesus Christ" (Jn 17: 3). This quotation, which begins the *Catechism of the Catholic Church,* places the reader in the presence of the mystery of God revealing himself to mankind, a theme which the Eastern Church has also given special place to in her theological developments as well as in her spirituality.

Although practically repeating the order of the chapters followed by the "old" (Roman) *Catechism* resulting from the Council of Trent and of a purely Western inspiration, the new one takes a perspective that is close to the mysticism of the Eastern traditions, for which knowledge of God is more the communion of all people with the Father through the Son in the Spirit, rather than a mere accumulation of statements and definitions about the articles of faith.

However, the "Western" stamp is still dominant in this new *Catechism* and that is understandable, as we shall see in the First Part. The "Eastern" imprint, however, is still visible, as we shall see in the Second Part; however, it will still remain necessary for the various Eastern Churches to inculturate the deposit of faith handed on in this *Catechism*, as we shall see in the Third Part.

The Catechism's Western stamp

The *Catechism* has an undeniable Western stamp, as can be seen by the number of explicit references to the Latin liturgy (88) compared with the 19 references to the Byzantine liturgies and three to the Syrian. In addition, the quotations from the Latin Fathers and other Western spiritual writers (309), particularly St. Augustine (88), are much more abundant than those from the Eastern Fathers and writers (158).

This quantitative choice can be attributed to a Western perspective that is dominant in the *Catechism.* Its theological vocabulary and major accents particularly emphasize the world of Western culture. Thus the mystery of faith is expressed more as "analogy" than as "apophatism" and the sense of "symbol" so dear to the Christian East (cf. *Catechism of the Catholic Church,* Part I, Section 1).

Then, too, in presenting the Christian faith it is the Apostles' Creed proclaimed during the baptismal ceremonies of the Church of Rome which has been chosen as the didactic framework over the Niceno-Constantinopolitan Creed which is the common reference of all the Eastern Churches (cf. Part I, Section 2).

In the explanation of the sacraments care was obviously taken to consider the Eastern traditions, especially those of the Byzantine rite. However, the points of reference are still the praxis and theology as found in the Roman ritual.

It is especially Part III, which treats of Christian morality, that is more distant from Oriental catechesis. If it had been more imbued with the spirit of the East, the section entitled "Life in Christ" would have presented this "life in Christ" as the "Church's existence" in the Holy Spirit with the Father and for the world. The perspective and expressions would have been more directly marked by the writings of the New Testament and patristic teaching.

This predominance of the Western perspective is not in the least surprising because the vast majority of people for whom the *Catechism* is intended belong to the cultural tradition which can be described as Western (Latin, Germanic, Anglo-Saxon, etc.). Then, too, there was limited Eastern representation on the

Commission of Cardinals and Archbishops (one out of 12) and on the editorial committee.

Such a lack of proportion was naturally discovered during the various consultations when the text was being drafted, especially during the broad consultation of the whole Catholic Episcopate (November 1989-May 1990).

Eastern imprint

However, one can say that, despite the clear predominance of the Western stamp in the text, the new *Catechism* attests to the "Church's catholicity" and "truly expresses what could be called the 'symphony' of faith" (John Paul II, Apostolic Constitution *Fidei Depositum*). This is not only because the Churches of all the continents participated actively in it, but also and more especially so, because the Eastern tradition itself is present in the Catholic Church as it has not been for a very long time. We should note, for example, that many amendments (*modi*), observations and comments inspired by the theology of the Christian East were introduced at the request of Bishops and experts who are not Eastern.

Credit, of course, is due to the Second Vatican Council, which invited the Church to breathe "with both lungs", East and West, as John Paul II has put it. The biblical, patristic, liturgical, spiritual and ecumenical renewal which the Council introduced and in which unspoken Eastern elements are also having an effect on Western expression, reflect Eastern theology's underlying but discernible presence in the *Catechism*.

In particular, we should point out the importance given to a theme that has pride of place for the Christian East: the knowledge of God as communion with the Father, through the Son and in the Spirit. This theme, as we have already mentioned in our introduction, is the *leitmotiv* running through the catechism's various developments.

This concept of meeting God in salvation history emphasizes the central place belonging to the incarnate Word, who died on the life-giving cross and rose for our salvation. In him we come to know the Father, and the mission of the Spirit (cf. nn. 683-741), a prolongation of the Son's, is made known to us. These especially Eastern perspectives form the framework the *Catechism* uses to proclaim the mystery of faith in the central explanation (creed) as well as in the other important sections (cf. Part II, Section 1 and Part IV, Section 1) or even in explaining the meaning of each sacrament (cf. Part V, Section 2).

As we have already said, this characteristically Eastern inspiration is absent from Part III. In contrast, however, Part IV, which deals with "Christian prayer", is thoroughly imbued with it. In an inclusive manner corresponding to the first sentence of the *Catechism* (Jn 17: 3), which affirms that eternal life is knowing the Father and Christ, prayer is said to be revealed through the various phases of the economy of salvation, handed on by the Church's Tradition, fulfilled in Christian life and hence integrated into the mystery of Christ. These points of view are characteristic of an authentically Eastern catechesis.

The final evidence of the Eastern tradition's influence on the *Catechism* is to be seen in the many references to the spiritual writers presented in smaller print. They are there less to prove the theological expressions than to support them with the experience that the Fathers of the whole Church have had of life in the Spirit; this attitude is also very Eastern.

Inculturation of the *Catechism* in The East

By the very fact that the *Catechism of the Catholic Church* is a "compendium of Catholic doctrine" and a "reference text" for local catechisms, an adaptation of its contents and method is necessary throughout the world, and so much more so for the Eastern Churches. Indeed, if the other Churches have to take into consideration the culture and mentality of their faithful, the theology expressed in the *Catechism* and which they must adapt, is theirs. On the contrary, as we have seen, the theological perspective proper to the East and already well articulated is still secondary in the *Catechism*.

Another characteristic of the inculturation of the *Catechism* which will need to be taken into consideration in the East is the multiplicity of traditions which, although very close to one another, have their own spiritual and theological visions. For example, it is necessary to recognize the impact of the Alexandrian school on the Copts, Ethiopians and even on the Armenians, as distinguished from the school of Antioch's impact on the Byzantines and Syrians. It is not merely a question of adapting cultures and mentalities, but of fidelity to centuries of theological traditions.

Among the practical measures common to these Churches of the East regarding the inculturation of the *Catechism*, it will obviously be necessary to restore to the Eucharistic liturgy celebrated by the Bishop (which is a living witness for the parish and the Diocese) the central place belonging to it in the catechesis of God's People. This tradition is still alive in some Eastern Churches.

A last question is raised concerning the East: at what point in passing on the new *Catechism of the Catholic Church* should this inculturation take place? Should it be carried out at the same time that the book is being translated into the various languages, or should it take place with the composition of local catechisms? If the first solution is chosen, it is not a question of changing the text; it will be faithfully translated. At the very most, one could add a supplement in which certain questions more characteristic of the Eastern tradition will be explained in the spirit of that tradition.

Conclusion

The realization of this *Catechism* attests to the Church's catholicity, also because so many voices (Bishops, theologians, exegetes, catechists) in harmony expressed what can be called a "symphony" of the faith (Apostolic Constitution *Fidei Depositum),* to which the inspiration of the Eastern tradition contributed in a real manner. The progress made on the path of universality in reflecting on it and cooperating in it is far from negligible. To make it grow, it will require more openness on the part of the West to the ancient Christian East, but also to all cultures; on the other hand, the East and its cultures must make a serious contribution to the common effort. The Second Vatican Council opened the door to such a communion of the Catholic Church in faith and the *Catechism* is one of its most visible fruits.

V

Catechism responds to desire and needs of Church today

by Cardinal Carlo M. Martini, S.J.
Archbishop of Milan, Italy

Some 2,000 years separate the Gospel and the *Catechism of the Catholic Church*. The number of years is irrelevant but what is significant is the great change that has marked the 2,000 years of history from the time of the Gospel to that of the new *Catechism*.

These years have seen many attempts to offer a concise, orderly and rational presentation of what Christians believe and by which they live. For this reason the new *Catechism* was based on the previous catechisms, just as the previous one drew on earlier attempts at synthesis, and so on, thus showing the structural dynamics linking the catechism to the Gospel or, more precisely, linking the originality of the catechism to the singularity of the Gospel.

The Gospel is, in fact, the "good news" of human salvation offered "once and for all" by the "messenger" of God, Jesus Christ: a definitive and therefore unique and unchangeable proclamation which will last until the end of time. From the Gospel's singularity comes the originality of the *Catechism*, which, on the one hand, must repeat the Gospel without adding or changing anything, but, on the other hand, must extract from the Gospel a synthesis of thought and action which form the essential basis of Christian life.

To avoid creating misunderstanding, it should be stated that the *Catechism* does not seek to "update" the Gospel because the Gospel *per se* is always contemporary; nor, for the same reason, can the catechism replace the Gospel; the Gospel and the catechism go together. The Gospel endures in its unsurpassable timeliness, while the catechism, with its humble but necessary function of adapting to historical circumstances which are transitory, takes on new life each time it is revised. Whereas the Gospel can never be outmoded or rewritten, the catechism needs to be updated periodically.

Message of faith is the Church's very soul

It was precisely the historical developments leading to the convoking of Vatican II that necessitated the publication of the *Catechism of the Catholic Church.* This is authoritatively stated by *Fidei Depositum,* the constitution with which Pope John Paul II promulgated it for the whole Church. Thus there is direct continuity between the Council and the *Catechism.* From this perspective, in fact, the *Catechism* can be added to the liturgical renewal and the new codification of canon law, to complete the *aggiornamento* called for by Pope John XXIII.

The reference to the Council takes us back in fact to the epoch-making changes which committed the Church to redefining herself in relation to the modern world. The impassioned question of Pope Paul VI, "Church, what do you say about yourself?", calls for a redefinition of the Church in her general principles (the Constitutions on the Church, *Lumen Gentium* and *Gaudium et Spes),* but also in her historical expressions of prayer (liturgical reform), legal discipline (revision of the Code of Canon Law), and lastly, the theory and practice of the faith.

Clearly the accomplishment of the last was the most arduous. In fact, more than in the other cases, it puts the Church in direct relationship with the world, making her part of its history. The message of faith, which the Church guards *(Fidei Depositum)* not as some object but rather as her own soul (which therefore constitutes her), is to be proclaimed to all people for their salvation. Estranged from the world and closed in on herself, the Church would lose her *raison d'être.*

Obviously this risk is not worth taking, especially not in this age of "secularization" or, as it has been called, the "post-Christian" world. In this perspective, secularization and hence, the modern world, is not to be considered a threat; for the Church it is rather to be seen as a challenge and incentive to "update" and, therefore, to reformulate the message of faith in the way that is most acceptable and persuasive in the current historical situation. From this awareness, came first Vatican II and now, as a logical result, the *Catechism of the Catholic Church*.

It is the result of assiduous research. In fact, the most remote preparatory stages were needed to support the final editorial phase. Spread over the whole postconciliar period, it saw all the "People of God" actively involved in a conscious search that not only involved redefining the manner of proclamation to non Christians, but, as a preliminary matter, the form of Christian understanding itself. It is not surprising that at times this research was confused and disordered. Every Christian has an active voice in the Church; but no Christian can claim the *charisma* of infallibility.

The *charisma* of the authentic interpretation of the Christian faith belongs only to the Pope and the Bishops in communion with him. The *Catechism of the Catholic Church* recalls this not only in its text, but even more explicitly in its desire to be in some way the "official" text of the Catholic Church. In any case, even apart from the formal question of its "official nature", the text is intended to perform the task, specific to the *Catechism*, of giving focus to the Church's self-awareness and mission in relation to her historical duties.

The historical duties of the Church are two. The first is always the same: evangelization; the second, ecumenical activity, derives from the painful, continuing separations that occur within the Church. With renewed awareness the Church is totality committed to it.

Church must take root in all cultures

The Church has taken note of her duty to evangelize and has added to her constant awareness of the unique saving power of the Gospel message for mankind her understanding of the newness produced by the emergence of new worlds and by the rise of cultures differing from those of Europe. Differentiating herself from European culture without rejecting it, and therefore remaining on her universal human foundation, the Church must take root in all cultures, transforming evangelization into inculturation.

The Church must seek a unity that accepts and appropriates legitimate differences, not a uniformity that cancels them. From this point of view, evangelization is faced with new problems, problems never encountered before in its history, because the correct solution, which must be found every time, often lies in striking a delicate balance between contrasting tendencies all claiming to be the only legitimate one.

As regards the "old" world, it too needs a "new evangelization", which is made all the more urgent by the obvious failure of all the ideologies which had claimed to take the place of the saving message of the Gospel.

The ecumenical task also seems new to the new Christian and Catholic sensitivity. Ecumenism represents a new era which has brought to a close the age of competition between Churches. It has brought the desire for reconciliation to maturity, leaving behind the desire for division and domination. The longing for unity tends to impose unity among the Churches as the primary requirement of the Spirit and, therefore, of Christian conscience.

Christian unity and, similarly, division among the Churches have always been proclaimed in the name of the truth: it is the truth that commands unity or that sanctions division; no Church can be prepared to re-establish unity at the cost of the truth, however professed. Evidently, the more sensitive they are to the ecumenical task, the more the drama of the Churches is reflected and multiplied in the consciousness of individual Christians. In this regard ecumenism, like inculturation, is seen not only as a source of difficulty, but as something problematic for the Christian conscience, which objectively requires enlightenment and direction.

Church's unity produced by faith

This very problem, which has caused even confusion and uncertainty in the conscience of Christians because of the newness of the duties to which they are called (and therefore apart from further motives of a subjective nature deriving from personal experience), explains to a great extent the sort of "*diaspora*" created within the "People of God" during the postconciliar period. The risk is that of the disintegration of the Christian conscience within the Church herself.

Once again, it is a risk that the Church cannot take without renouncing her identity and vocation as "guardian of the faith". The Church's unity in fact is fundamentally produced by faith: if her unity is broken it is because in some way its principle is under discussion, that is to say, the faith is questioned.

Thus the specific reason for, and hence the particular purpose of the *Catechism of the Catholic Church is* apparent. It is meant to clarify what it means to believe, that is, to reformulate the faith in its "objectivity" in order to restore unity to the "People of God". The newness of the cultural changes and the historical duties which the "People of God" must assume do not legitimize either a "*diaspora*" within the "People of God" nor, correspondingly, the fragmentation of the faith; on the contrary, they demand that unity which the objectivity of a faith recognized and professed alone can produce.

VI

Catechism offers prospects for ecumenical reflection

by Fr. Max Thurian
International Theological Commission

The search for the visible unity of Christians requires an ecumenical dialogue based on a frank and clear witness to the truths of the faith. Unity is not achieved in doctrinal confusion or in seeking the lowest common denominator. The visible unity of Christians can be founded only on the full truth understood in doctrinal clarity and fraternal charity.

Following the Second Vatican Council, theological dialogue between the Catholic Church and the various Christian communions has sought to follow this method of clarity in openness, and it has already succeed in achieving important results. However, in order to lay the cornerstone of the Catholic doctrinal position, it was sometimes necessary to refer to various sources in Tradition, and it was not always easy for theologians to reach agreement on the importance of one or other of the documents of the Magisterium. The lack was often felt of a reference text in which one could find the full, unequivocal teaching of the Catholic Church in all its homogeneous development, including the important stage of Vatican II.

The *Catechism of the Catholic Church* fills this gap and enables the reader to know the Catholic doctrine about all the important points of the faith. It will therefore be a valuable aid to ecumenical dialogue, where it is always necessary to know the positions of each partner in order to discern convergence or note differences with total clarity and honesty. Many pages of the *Catechism* will show a community of faith among Christians, particularly in the First Section concerning the profession of faith in God, the Father, Son and Holy Spirit, and in the final part on Christian prayer.

Certain delicate points in ecumenical dialogue are, in the *Catechism*, clarified sufficiently to clear up all misunderstandings, so much so that when the truth is expressed with complete clarity and according to its full traditional and biblical dimension, it is more readily convincing. One could cite many examples, but here we must limit ourselves to some of the main topics of ecumenical dialogue.

An important position is given to the Scriptures in the *Catechism*, which constantly quotes them as a basis for its affirmations. "Scripture and Tradition flowing out from the same divine well-spring, come together in some fashion to form one thing, and move towards the same goal" (n. 80, cf. *Dei Verbum*, n. 9).

The Church's certitude is summarized in the "In brief", n. 135: "Since they are inspired by God, . . . the Scriptures . . . present God's own Word in an unalterable form" (*Dei Verbum,* n. 24). The Church encourages all Christians to acquire a deep knowledge of Jesus Christ by frequent reading of the Scriptures. Indeed, "ignorance of the Scriptures is ignorance of Christ" (n. 133, quoting St. Jerome and *Dei Verbum,* n. 25).

Catholic Church contains full means of salvation

Before explaining the Creed, the *Catechism* shows that salvation comes from God alone and is communicated to us through the faith handed on to us by the Church, our Mother. "We believe the Church to be the mother of our new birth but not the author of our salvation. Because she is our mother, she is also responsible for educating us in the faith" (n. 169, quoting Faustus of Riez). God's grace awakens in us the faith which attaches us to Christ: "Moved by the grace of the Holy Spirit and drawn to the Father, we believe and confess concerning Jesus: 'You are the Christ, the Son of the living God' (Mt 16: 16). It is on the rock of this faith, confessed by St. Peter, that Christ has built his Church" (n. 424, quoting St. Leo the Great).

As for the one, holy, catholic and apostolic Church, the *Catechism* draws from the teaching of Vatican II and in particular its Decree on Ecumenism. "This Church alone as a society established and organized in the world, subsists in *(subsistit in)* the Catholic Church governed by Peter's Successor and the Bishops who are in communion with him" (n. 816). It is through her that "the fullness of the means of salvation can be obtained" *(Unitatis Redintegratio n. 3)*.

However, regarding those who are born today into communities separated from the Catholic Church but who live the faith in Christ, "the Catholic Church accepts them with fraternal respect and affection as brothers . . .. It remains true that those who have been justified by faith in Baptism are incorporated into Christ; they therefore have a right to be called Christians and with good reason are accepted as brothers by the children of the Catholic Church" *(Unitatis Redintegratio* n. 3).

In addition, "many elements of sanctification and of truth" *(Lumen Gentium,* n. 8) "are found outside her visible confines . . .. Christ's Spirit uses these Churches and ecclesial communities as a means of salvation, whose efficacy derives from the fullness of grace and truth that Christ entrusted to the Catholic Church. All these gifts come from Christ and lead to him (cf. *Unitatis Redintegratio,* n. 3) and of themselves call for "Catholic unity" *(Lumen Gentium,* n. 8)" (nn. 818-819). The whole concept of Vatican II's Catholic ecumenism is contained in this phrase.

The *Catechism* also provides a "programme" for ecumenical work which will one day achieve the visible unity of Christians, and which includes the following elements: permanent renewal of the Church; conversion of heart in order to live the Gospel better; prayer in common mutual fraternal knowledge; ecumenical training; theological dialogue; meetings between Christians; cooperation in the service of humanity (n. 821).

In the chapter on the sacraments of Christian initiation, Baptism is called "the sacred bond of Christian unity" (n. 1271), in conformity with Vatican II *(Unitatis Redintegratio,* n. 22). This sacrament is the basis of communion among all Christians, including those who are not yet in full communion with the Catholic Church. Thus, with Vatican II the *Catechism* confirms that although communion among all Christians is imperfect, it has a sacramental nature through the common Baptism which incorporates them into a community of life in the Body of Christ. This represents the great progress made by ecumenism and the promise of an ever greater unity.

As for the Eucharist, the *Catechism* has been able to combine the traditional doctrine of the Fathers and of the Council of Trent with the biblical enrichment of the liturgical renewal that prepared for Vatican II. Ecumenical dialogue on Baptism, the Eucharist and the ministry, continued over the past few years by the Faith and Order Commission of the World Council of Churches in Geneva, with the active participation of Catholic theologians, has paved the way for greater unity in the faith.

The Catholic Church has made an official, constructive response to this universal dialogue, unique in history. The traditional Catholic doctrine expressed by the *Catechism* shows how much progress has been achieved over the past few years in theological reflection on the Eucharist, and especially on "the sacramental sacrifice: thanksgiving, commemoration, presence" (nn. 1356-1381).

Many points of agreement regarding prayer

The Catholic Church recognizes her doctrinal communion with the Orthodox Churches in regard to the Eucharist and the priesthood, which enables her to envisage "a certain communion *in sacris"* (n. 1399). Eucharistic intercommunion is not possible with the ecclesial communities that were a consequence of the Reformation because of divergences concerning the sacrament of Orders, the priesthood and the episcopate (cf. n. 1400).

However, the Church foresees, in certain cases, that Catholic ministers can administer the Eucharist to other Christians who are not in full communion with the Catholic Church and who spontaneously request it, on condition that they show a Catholic faith in the Eucharist and have the necessary dispositions (cf. n.

1401). In this way the Church wishes at the same time to show her maternal generosity and her faithful attentiveness to the doctrine of the priesthood and the sacraments.

The sections which deal with "life in Christ" and "Christian prayer" will stimulate common Christian reflection: personal freedom, moral conscience, faith and grace, the tradition of prayer, Sunday worship, etc. On many points ecumenical dialogue will be able to demonstrate Christian agreement.

On points that still create problems in ecumenical dialogue, the *Catechism* also offers promising prospects for stimulating reflection. This is the case with Mary's role in Christian prayer. We like to quote this lovely text:

"Mary is the perfect *orans,* a figure of the Church. When we pray to her, we are adhering with her to the plan of the Father who sent his Son to save all humanity. Like the beloved disciple, we make our own (cf. Jn 19: 27) the Mother of Jesus, who has become the mother of all the living. We can pray with her and to her. The prayer of the Church is borne, as it were, on the prayer of Mary. She is united with the Church in hope (cf. *Lumen Gentium* nn. 68-69)" (n. 2679).

Is it not possible that this *Catechism of the Catholic Church* can be for all Christian communions, in all freedom, an occasion for them to verify their faith and deepen their understanding of God's word? This would be an ecumenical service that the *Catechism* could fulfill with a view to the visible unity of all Christians for which Christ prayed ardently.

VII

Inculturation of the Catechism at the local level is necessary

by Cardinal José T. Sánchez
Prefect of the Congregation for the Clergy

One of the purposes of the *Catechism of the Catholic Church* is to be a reliable and authentic reference for the drafting of diocesan and national catechisms, whose mediation is indispensable (cf. Address of John Paul II, 25 June 1992).

It is not intended as a substitute for local, duly approved catechisms, but to encourage and assist in the drafting of new ones, which should take into account different situations and cultures and take pains to safeguard the fidelity and unity of Catholic doctrine (cf. Apostolic Constitution *Fidei Depositum,* n. 4).

However, although the *Catechism of the Catholic Church* requires further inculturation on the local level, it should be considered a successful attempt at an inculturation of faith and a catechetical re-expression of the Christian message at the level of the universal Church. It can and must be considered an exemplary way of reformulating in today's global culture the documents of Revelation and Christian tradition, particularly those of Vatican II. Of course, it is not the only possible nor perhaps even the best way; but it is a reliable guide for Bishops, theologians, catechist instructors and catechists who are facing the arduous task of inculturating the faith and catechesis in a first and general approximation.

"There are many links between the message of salvation and culture. In his self-revelation to his people culminating in the fullness of manifestation in his incarnate Son, God spoke according to the culture proper to each age. Similarly the Church has existed through the centuries in varying circumstances and has utilized the resources of different cultures in her preaching to spread and explain the message of Christ, to examine and understand it more deeply, and to express it more perfectly in the liturgy and in various aspects of the life of the faithful.

"Nevertheless, the Church has been sent to all ages and nations and, therefore, is not tied exclusively and indissolubly to any race or nation, to any one particular way of life, or to any customary practices ancient or modern. The Church is faithful to her traditions and is at the same time conscious of her universal mission; she can, then, enter into communion with different forms of culture, thereby enriching both herself and the cultures themselves" *(Gaudium et Spes,* n. 58).

The *Catechism of the Catholic Church* "is a statement of the Church's faith and of Catholic doctrine attested or illumined by Sacred Scripture, by the Apostolic Tradition and by the Church's Magisterium" *(Fidei Depositum,* n. 4).

Necessary adaptation left to appropriate catechisms

"The emphasis of this *Catechism* is on doctrinal explanation. Indeed, it is intended to help people deepen their knowledge of the faith. Precisely for this reason it is directed to maturing this faith, to implanting it in life and to spreading it through witness.

"Because of its intrinsic finality, this *Catechism* does not intend to undertake adaptations of the explanation and the catechetical methods demanded by differences of culture, age, spiritual life and the social and ecclesial situation of those to whom the *Catechism* is addressed. These indispensable adaptations are left to the appropriate catechisms, and still more, to those who instruct the faithful" (Preface, nn. 23-24).

However, one can reasonably foresee that in adapting the *Catechism* to the various categories of those to whom it is addressed, distinguished by their age, spiritual life, type of culture and sociological and ecclesial background, certain difficulties could arise. Here are two fairly substantial ones which eventually should be faced and resolved with sound realism, in their respective contexts:

- The first can be expressed as follows: since it would be difficult to adapt the *Catechism* to local situations mainly because of its pronounced doctrinal style, it would end up being used directly as a catechetical text. The *Catechism of the Catholic Church* would thus gradually take the place of existing national, regional and diocesan catechisms; it would stop those in the process of being drafted, consequently crushing the catechetical renewal promoted these past few years by the Episcopates in the various local Churches.

- The second difficulty touches the crux of the current catechetical debate and concerns the definition and description of the term "catechism". Referring to *Catechesi Tradendæ*, n. 50, and to the *General Catechetical Directory*, n. 119, it can be reduced to the following question: is the *Catechism* a doctrinal compendium that lacks the basic elements of an up-to-date methodology and pedagogy?

The differences in this regard among those who teach catechists are well known. Some feel that the incarnational/inculturational aspect is essential to the *Catechism*. According to them, the objective content of doctrine should be correlated and adapted to the conditions of those being catechized; a catechism cannot be a mere doctrinal compendium ignoring the worries, needs, expectations and problems of the particular people to whom it is addressed. In the wake of the *General Catechetical Directory* and *Catechesi Tradendæ*, they hold that the text should be doubly faithful: to God and to human beings. Issues such as justice, peace, ecology, freedom, solidarity and equality should play an important role in the text.

According to this trend, an up-to-date methodology which includes the use of the human sciences (especially those of pedagogy and modern communications), and therefore a language, style and structural composition appropriate for those for whom it is intended is not an extrinsic element of a catechism but its essential element, without which the text would be abstract and dull.

Those who promote this view should however have no difficulty in accommodating their position to the intentions and goals of the *Catechism.*

Guidelines for mediation to be set by Congregation

There is a second trend among catechist instructors, a small but significant number of whom emphasize Catholic doctrine as the unique and essential content of the catechism, while leaving to the catechists and their catechetical materials (not to catechisms) the task of inculturating and incarnating the message.

They maintain that the catechism should deal more with the norms of teaching *(Lehrnorm)* than with its form *(Lehrform)* and that the more methodological and pedagogical elements the catechism contains, the more it loses its catechetical identity.

This trend recognizes necessary methodological adjustments in the sense that all teaching should take its audience into account, but prefers to see the catechism strictly as a presentation of the essential content of faith. It is up to catechists and their didactic materials to present the message in an incarnational way.

In accordance with their position, the supporters of this line will correctly maintain that with the *Catechism of the Catholic Church* the authentic, authoritative catechism has finally arrived, the *regula fidei,* the sure and no longer disputable measure of orthodoxy. But not a few of them will also claim, but no longer correctly, that there is no need for local catechisms to serve as an intermediary of the *Catechism of the Catholic Church.*

According to these people, this means the content of a catechism does not require an appropriate doctrinal and methodological framework to achieve its purpose. Method and inculturation itself are ensured above all by the faith and consistent life of the catechist. In living the faith personally and socially, communicators of the faith make it part of the culture and therefore put themselves in the position of transmitting to catechumens a Christian truth that has already been inculturated.

Moreover, quite a number of them hope that the basic textbook for catechists, especially at the primary level, will consist of the final summaries of each chapter of the *Catechism of the Catholic Church* (the "in briefs") because, among other reasons, the direct use of the entire text, which is voluminous and markedly theological, would be difficult.

In perspective, supporters of this second view would have an easy time in countries where catechetical structures are not developed to the point of producing local catechisms; and also in cat-echetically developed countries where it is impossible to produce national catechisms because of great social and cultural disparity among the various regions that form the country. But these could be the objective source of tension in countries where the Bishops and Episcopal Conferences have for some time been developing organic catechetical plans including official catechisms for specific age groups or social and ecclesial categories.

These difficulties and other possible ones create for the Congregation for the Clergy, which has responsibility for catechetics, the pastoral necessity of setting guidelines to direct the right mediation and inculturation of the *Catechism of the Catholic Church* in local catechisms. In this undertaking, however, it is not starting from scratch. Criteria and guides for the drafting and assessment of diocesan and national catechisms are easily found in the documents of the post-conciliar catechetical Magisterium, especially in the *General Catechetical Directory* and in *Catechesi Tradendœ*.

A summary list follows, preceded by two obvious remarks:

- the *Catechism of the Catholic Church* and its mediation must be placed in the context and wake of the *General Catechetical Directory* and *Catechesi Tradendœ;*

- the *Catechism of the Catholic Church* and its mediation are to be coordinated with the catechetical ministry of a diocese, a region or a nation.

And here are the criteria that determine the drafting and assessment of a local catechism:

- Scripture, Tradition and the Magisterium as sources (*General Catechetical Directory,* nn. 37, 45; *Catechesi Tradendœ,* nn. 27, 52);

- inculturation of the message *(General Catechetical Directory,* n. 37; *Catechesi Tradendæ,* n. 53; *Evangelii Nuntiandi,* n. 63);
- integrity, organic unity and arrangement of the contents *(General Catechetical Directory,* nn. 38-39; *Catechesi Tradendæ,* nn. 21, 30; *Evangelii Nuntiandi,* nn. 32, 65);
- plurality of methods *(General Catechetical Directory,* n. 46; *Catechesi Tradendæ,* n. 55);
- pedagogical uniqueness of catechesis *(Catechesi Tradendæ,* n. 58);
- memorization of "in brief" formulæ *(Catechesi Tradendæ,* n. 55);
- style, plan and proposals; adoption of popular piety *(Catechesi Tradendæ,* n. 54);
- Christocentrism *(Dei Verbum,* n. 2; *General Catechetical Directory* 40, 52; *Evangelii Nuntiandi,* n. 27; *Catechesi Tradendæ,* n. 5ff.);
- trinitarian theocentrism *(General Catechetical Directory,* n. 41);
- hierarchy of truths *(Unitatis Redintegratio,* n. 11; *General Catechetical Directory,* n. 43);
- mystery of salvation as history *(General Catechetical Directory,* n. 44; *Catechesi Tradendæ,* n. 44);
- reference to the creeds, *(Catechesi Tradendæ,* n. 28);
- correlation between faith and life *(General Catechetical Directory,* nn. 26, 38, 63-64, *Evangelii Nuntiandi,* nn. 29, 31; *Catechesi Tradendæ, n. 29);*
- ecumenical dimension *(General Catechetical Directory,* n. 27; *Catechesi Tradendæ,* n. 32-34);
- liturgical dimension *(General Catechetical Directory,* n. 25, *Catechesi Tradendæ,* n. 23),
- missionary dimension *(Evangelii Nuntiandi,* nn. 14-15, *Catechesi Tradendæ,* nn. 10-13, 15-16, 62-66, 71; *Redemptoris Missio,* n. 73);
- eschatological dimension *(General Catechetical Directory,* nn. 29, 69);

- witness for the acceptance of contents *(Evangelii Nuntiandi,* n. 21; *General Catechetical Directory,* n. 35; *Redemptoris Missio,* n. 42).

The criteria/guidelines listed are certainly also useful in inculturating the *Catechism of the Catholic Church* in local catechisms, but on close examination, they appear not to have been specifically designed for that purpose.

In fact, such criteria seem inadequate for solving questions of this kind: how can the *Catechism of the Catholic Church* be *a concrete* reference point for local catechisms? What does "reference" mean for catechesis and catechisms in the various catechetical and cultural contexts?

Or in greater detail: given that the *General Catechetical Directory* considers the human sciences (anthropological as well as didactic and pedagogical) as resources enabling a catechism to achieve the greatest possible approximation between the one divine message and various cultures (cf. *General Catechetical Directory* nn. 37, 119) some ask: is it possible to fix for each ethnic and cultural area a correct "dose" of human knowledge to be included in the catechisms, so that they provide suitable mediation for the *Catechism of the Catholic Church* on the local level?

In particular, as regards the science of language and communications, what precise criteria can be suggested so that local catechisms can transmit with ease the whole content, without any distortion to the different recipients of today, not only children, adolescents, young people and adults, but also the disabled, intellectuals, workers?

Certainly the genius and creativity of pastors, catechists and local communities, with the grace of the Holy Spirit, will find ways to inculturate the *Catechism of the Catholic Church* in their respective countries. But the preceding questions and others concerning particularly the degree of preparation of those who impart catechesis, explain the initiative taken by the Congregation for the Clergy last November, to initiate an exchange of reflections with the Presidents of the Episcopal Commissions for Catechesis, in order to identify more specific criteria for the mediation of this *Catechism* and for relevant pastoral practice. Furthermore, also profiting from the contribution in this regard that will be made by the members of the International Council for Catechesis, the Dicastery intends to provide guidelines to ensure a good reception and a proper use of the *Catechism* in the local Churches.

VIII

Introduction to new Catechism highlights the centrality of faith

by Alessandro Maggiolini
Bishop of Como, Italy

Our intention is to comment on the First Section of the First Part of the *Catechism of the Catholic Church*. To comment on, that is, to extract the fundamental aspects of the exposition, leaving to the direct reading of the text the analytical absorption of the contents.

Although inserted into the *corpus* of the *Catechism*, these pages serve as an introduction. They examine primarily the act of—or the virtue of—faith in the human subject who is a member of the Church, that is to say, the *fides qua*. All the rest of the magisterial document will be a presentation of the "object "of the act of faith, the *fides quæ*.

It seems superfluous to point out the importance of this introduction which identifies decisive passages which are valid for the entire work.

Preliminary remarks

A priori we might have expected an introductory guide to the act of faith: a kind of synthesis of "fundamental theology" or of "apologetics".

But this is not the case. The book contains references to the great themes proper to such a level of inquiry: the "natural" knowability of God as the beginning and end of all things, miracles, prophecies, the propagation of Christianity, the holiness of the Church, etc., as "certain signs" of revealed truth, etc. But, since it is addressed primarily to believers, it looks at all of these certitudes and many others, in the light of faith. The task of laying the rational foundations of belief is delegated to various disciplines. If anything, a kind of implicit "threshold apologetics" is used in describing Christianity as responding to a person's deepest yearning and as a religion of enormous aesthetic appeal.

In this sense the point of view adopted does not, to be sure, disdain truth in itself, attainable through the capacities of the human mind alone; but it pays special attention to the unfolding of history, of a history seen with the eyes of faith.

Thus, a Christocentrism is immediately evident in the document. Creation has the Lord Jesus, the incarnate Word who died and rose, as its efficient, exemplary and final cause. Without pressing this view too much, hardening it into a theological "thesis", following clear indications in the statements of Vatican II, there is little attempt made to consider the design of providence as if it were twofold: one "natural" to which another "supernatural" one would be added; the divine plan is one and has as its centre Christ, through whom and in view of whom everything has been created.

In this context, historical man has never been in a condition of "pure nature": created in grace, he sinned; but God never ceases to call him to fellowship of thought and life with himself. This means that man does not have two ends to which he must tend: he has but one vocation which is of the supernatural order, in the attainment of which he also fulfill his dimension as a creature.

To say that man is a "religious being" does not imply merely an opposition to atheistic outlooks in the form of scientific or "ascetic" postulates in the acceptance of his own finiteness; it also amounts to sustaining that the "restless heart" is preconditioned by grace which wants it to be satisfied only in the God of Jesus Christ: whether man knows it or not, this is his orientation.

Thus, as has already been said, salvation has a dialogical structure—or one related to covenant—through which God offers himself and man is called to receive him freely in order to become one with the Father, through Christ, in the Spirit.

We speak of the human person, a sinner but yet drawn to rise above himself through divine mercy: the human person who enters into the religious relationship not only with his intellect, but also by the strength of his will, feelings, etc.

We speak of the human person as inserted into a context of sin and hence of isolation and solitude; yet he is called to enter into the communion of the Church, and, indeed, is saved precisely by this communion.

God reveals himself and gives himself

The dialogue of redemption is initiated by God who creates in order to redeem. Man is already gift in his very being because he was made to exist, but he is also the product of another and greater gift because he has been liberated from his sins and made to share in the life of God.

It is a question of a continuous and gradual initiative that reaches all human beings who live in diverse historical situations.

God, in a sense, makes himself present in the human condition so as to redeem it, as it were, from within and bring it to fulfillment.

By an irrevocable oath, God remains at the heart of the human situation and intensifies his presence: at first his presence has a general and germinal intent; then it becomes word and action which jointly save through the mediation of chosen individuals; in the fullness of time, the Word becomes flesh in Jesus of Nazareth, dwells among us, dies and rises in order to remain with us in his very reality as a divine Person who also takes on a human nature transfigured in the Paschal mystery.

After Christ there is no further public revelation. But it is worth stressing the fact that, with the Lord Jesus, that which—or rather, the One who—is offered to humanity is not merely the truth about God expressed in human words and the redemptive dynamism of God's will expressed in human deeds, but rather God himself, as Father, who sends the Son so that he can give us the gift of the Spirit.

This is the richness of the universal sacrament of the Church in which Christ is present wherever two or more are gathered in his name, wherever the Scriptures are proclaimed, wherever the sacraments, and especially the Eucharist, are celebrated.

The primitive community, following the mind of its Founder, is structured as a mediation in which the Apostles, with Peter and subject to Peter, have the task of teaching according to norms, of celebrating the sanctifying rites and of guiding the faithful in the way of holiness.

The Church continues, then, until Christ returns, her instrumental tasks, summoning everyone to a shared responsibility which must be total in its intensity, but diverse in the manner of participation.

In the light of these reminders, and with special attention to the truth component to be interpreted, transmitted and spread, one can see how the Church becomes a kind of channel by which the Spirit of Christ spurs to action.

One begins to see too the relationship between Tradition and Scripture. Tradition can also be some aspect of unwritten truth, but it is above all the Church herself that originally experienced life with Christ and in some way and to some degree continues to experience it.

Scripture, especially the New Testament, is as it were the crystallization of part of what the sacred writers saw and touched of the Word of life and which they narrated under the inspiration of the Holy Spirit. In this sense Scripture is in its very origin in some way part of the living Tradition which becomes fixed in the written word. It then becomes a normative moment of reference to help us understand—ever more but never totally—what God has revealed in his Son: what God has manifested in an explicit written and/or oral manner and what is necessarily connected with this. (Is it really superfluous to add that the "word of God" which is treated by Vatican II is the whole of revelation and not Scripture alone?)

It seems useful to illustrate the Scripture's function in its interpretative phase. Obviously, the objective revealed datum does not increase. What increases is rather one's comprehension of it through human understanding and spiritual penetration: the penetration, that is, which is accomplished in the light of and under the inspiration of the Spirit, the same Spirit who guided the writing of the Bible.

It will come as no surprise that a reading in faith is able to discover even what Scripture does not say openly since the "good Book" offers a general vision of God, of man and of the world in the light of the faith which, in the one plan of salvation, also includes the created component (including "natural" ethics in the sense indicated).

It will also come as no surprise that the deepening and growth of the understanding of revelation is not an exclusively magisterial affair. The "simple" believers with the *sensus fidei*, in a kind of innate knowledge can find new intuitions of the divine truth, and, indeed, are infallible in this task, so long as they are in union with the Church's hierarchy.

Similarly, theologians can reach "new" awareness of revelation through the scholarly study of the same (without however forgetting that even theologians are called to be faithful). The Magisterium will then have the function of confirming believers; and it will do this by engaging in various ways and degrees— also in accordance with historical situations—the authority of Christ in whose name it teaches.

The Magisterium's teaching normally takes place in an occasional way: adhering to the desires of authentic Christians, clarifying disputed points of doctrine, recalling forgotten aspects of revelation, etc. Various ways of organizing the content of the faith are called for in various contexts and for various ends.

In the case of a *Catechism* which is meant to be an organic and complete exposition of the revealed truth, it will be necessary to take into account in a very special manner the so-called "hierarchy of truths": a hierarchy which is not to be confused with the level of authority which the Magisterium has adopted in various cases, but is to be viewed as a matter of the closeness or distance from the centre of a synthesis, which can only be Christ, the One sent by the Father who gives the gift of the Spirit.

Man responds

The priority of God in the dialogue of faith is not only revealed in the offer of Christ, but also in a way that is interior to man, whom the Spirit prepares for the decision to believe. In fact, when grace finds the person open, it establishes in that person the moral conditions which will enable his will and his intellect to adhere to God.

Faith is not merely the act of giving credence to a number of affirmations on the authority of a God who reveals. It is also the adherence of the person's whole being to God who offers himself in the Lord Jesus and who anticipates the act of the human person by "raising" his mind and will to participate in the knowledge and love of Christ.

Such an abandonment to God, which is the fruit of grace, rescues man. In this sense, faith does not deny but accepts, purifies and perfects the human intellect and will. The mind prepares the act of faith and is stimulated by belief itself. The will makes the decision to believe, but is also reinforced by the act of faith. The emotional component itself, at least in part, can dispose one to faith, but, within certain limits, it is also healed and assumed in an ordered fashion into the synthesis of the person by the choice of faith.

Even the response to the dialogue on the part of the believer takes place within the Church. The Church is in fact a "proof" of the revealed realities; it is the community which, inhabited by Christ and by the Spirit, presents itself as the "place" of the "object" and the mystery of the "subject" of faith; it is the agency which educates the Christian personality in its fullness. The "I believe", in a certain sense, emerges from the "we believe", where the "we" is ultimately the Lord Jesus with the communion of saints.

As has been said, faith is called to grow to perfection where it acts in charity.

The act of belief is a "reasonable" act; it has sufficient intellectual motivation but does not possess motives that force a decision, since the latter is born of freedom supported by grace. In a certain sense one can affirm that the external and internal call of God explains the necessity of believing freely, because only in this way is man himself as he should be according to the design of providence into which he is admitted.

The act of the believer does not terminate at the words or at the idea but at the very reality of Christ. This helps us to understand also the value of the terminological and conceptual dimension of the profession of faith which enables a unique unity in the particular Church and in the universal Church. (The *Catechism* is an example of this.)

The act of believing in its fullness not only explains revelation's influence on the believer's personal life but it also leads him to praise God and to evangelize. The Creed, in fact, is an act of adoration and it is the norm of the Christian's mission, although attention and dedication to the poor also cannot be neglected.

Faith, we have seen, already depends in some way on the reality of Christ. It is however destined to relinquish the entire *enuntiabile* in order to achieve the *res* in eternal bliss, but not without experiencing even through earthly life, a certain *prælibatio* of what will be, beyond time, in the fullness of joy and in the end that has no end.

IX

Catechism beautifully illustrates the nature of liturgical action

by Estanislao Esteban Karlic
Archbishop of Paraná, Argentina

In a marvelous sequence of ideas expressing the harmony of revealed truth and the real unity of the divine plan, the *Catechism* treats the celebration of the Christian mystery in Part II, having treated the revelation of this mystery in Part I.

In the drafting of this section particular attention was given to preserving the proportion of the four great blocks into which the text is divided, and a well balanced result was achieved. Although liturgical celebration is at the center of the Church's life, it occupies only 23% of the text, while the profession of faith takes up 39%. It is striking that in the *Roman Catechism* of the Council of Trent, the proportions are reversed: 37% for the sacraments and 22% for the treatment of the creed. There are historical reasons which can help to explain this fact: at Trent it was necessary to defend the sacramental order with great firmness since it had been considerably weakened in the thinking the Protestant Reformation; to the world of today, however, the need is to teach fully and insistently the integrity of revealed truth, which is being silenced by secularism and questioned by relativism.

In accordance with sound doctrine, and in line with Vatican II (cf. *Sacrosanctum Concilium,* n. 10), the *Catechism* stresses that the liturgy is the culmination of the life of the People of God. This very important understanding, which characterizes Catholicism, is expressed quite vividly in this part, in the First Section which deals with the "sacramental economy" in general (nn. 1076—1134) and in the second, which is devoted to the sacraments in particular (nn. 1135-1209). Here we will discuss the First Section.

The sacramental economy

With doctrinal precision and stylistic beauty, the text of the *Catechism* illustrates the nature of liturgical action, above all of the sacraments which form its center, and the newness characteristic of sacramental celebration.

Christ the Lord, who saves us primarily through his Passover, institutes the Church, his Mystical Body, which born from his open side on the cross, is revealed at Pentecost and begins her mediating mission as the universal sacrament of salvation. Basically through the liturgy the Church is a sign and an instrument of the saving work of Jesus Christ.

The liturgy is an action pertaining to the Blessed Trinity. It is the work of the Father who through his Son and the Spirit, continues the realization of his plan. Through it God fulfills his plan which, passing through the Paschal mystery of Christ from creation to the end of time, is an immense divine blessing to which responds the blessing of the human person who acknowledges it and gives thanks for it, offering in turn to the Lord the gifts received.

The liturgy is likewise the work of the Church, the sacrament of Christ the Savior. When the time of the Church was inaugurated at Pentecost, the sacramental economy began: the administration of salvation will be wholly a trinitarian and ecclesial work at the same time. Rightly then are the sacraments called the sacraments of Christ and the Church.

Liturgical celebration is a wonderful interweaving of signs and symbols. How are they composed? Since everything comes from God and was created through Christ and for him (cf. Jn 1: 3; Col 1: 16), all of nature can be used by God to manifest his blessing that sanctifies people and the blessing of men who praise God. In the sacraments, water, oil, bread and wine are used, as are other signs and symbols of human culture: washing, anointing, eating and drinking, imposition of hands. Their natural meaning was brought nearer to the mystery of redemption through the Old Testament and have acquired their full significance in Christ, by whom the sacraments were instituted as a sign and cause of the new life of grace.

Inasmuch as they are signs of Christ who accomplishes redemption, they are efficacious in virtue of the very acts performed: *ex opere operato*. Because they are human signs, their significance must be definite and authentic and must be lived with truth through the faith of all the participants: they are sacraments of faith. The sacraments, instituted by Jesus Christ, were received through the Apostles. For this reason the expression *"lex orandi, lex credendi"* is valid when applied to the liturgy and means that one must believe what the prayer expresses.

Liturgical celebration is the operative presence of the risen Christ who continues his work of redemption. The truth of the resurrection of the Lord is the basis of the liturgy's realism. It does not consist in purely symbolic ceremonies, but through them and in them the Lord of glory, Jesus Christ, is present to communicate the life of his grace and to make human beings true children of God.

The liturgy is the "celebration of the Christian mystery", its actualization which enables individuals and successive generations to participate in its holiness and to prepare themselves for glory. The risen Christ is real, his Sacramental action in the Church is real, and his effect in the hearts of the participating faithful renewed in the Lord is real.

The Catechism's service is not only in professing the truth about the mystery of Christ, but also in presenting the sacraments as "God's masterpieces" through which the mystery—communicated and received with a grateful heart—teaches us to live the Lord's law of love, imitating him in his giving of himself even unto death.

The *Catechism* strongly underscores the fact that the liturgy which we celebrate on earth places us in communion with the eternal liturgy, in which everything is communion and celebration of God with the angels and saints. The whole pilgrim Church participates in this celebration because all the baptized are ordained through the universal priesthood to the praise of the grace of God (cf. *Lumen Gentium,* n. 10), each according to his function, and that in this hierarchical communion the service proper to pastors is exercised by the successors of the Apostles, the Bishops, and by the priests, their coworkers, who are ordained to act in the name of Christ, the Head of his people: *in persona Christi capitis* (cf. *Presbyterorum Ordinis,* nn. *2-5).*

The *Catechism* underscores the festive character of the liturgy. The liturgy enables the Church to share in the glory of Christ. It is thus a celebration par excellence, because a celebration's dimension is proportionate to the reason for celebrating, and there is no greater good than that of being incorporated into Christ through the action of the Holy Spirit to the glory of God the Father. Thus through the liturgy we are introduced into the liturgy of the heavenly Church, into the feast at which God the Father presides on his throne, together with his Son Jesus Christ, the eternal High Priest, and the Holy Spirit, who sanctifies people like the purest water (cf. Rv 22: 17).

The liturgy will serve then to fulfill the need in the spiritual life for a legitimate, pure joy which is sought by many who unfortunately become involved in sects, where they hope to find it. Man is called to rejoice in the Paschal mystery of Christ. "If Christ be not risen, then your faith is vain" (1 Cor 15: 17). Christianity is a joyous reality through participation in the Pasch of Christ.

The 'today' of liturgy

Christ's resurrection and ascension into heaven usher in a new era. From that time on the Paschal mystery accomplished once for all in the history of humanity sows in that history a seed of eternity, the life of grace, the beginning of glory, and the relationship of the glorious Christ with all times as their Lord begins. In Christ the eternal now begins. Saint Hippolytus, cited by the *Catechism,* brilliantly expresses this idea: " . . . for us who believe in him (Christ), there begins a day of light, long, eternal, which never ends: the mystical Passover" (*Pasc.* 1-2).

He is the one whom the liturgy recalls, lives and celebrates today, he who urges people to come and take possession of the life that never ends. The liturgy is not only a memorial *(anamnesis)* but also an invocation of the Spirit *(epiklesis)* to make the Paschal mystery present. The *anamnesis* and the *epiklesis* are the heart of the liturgical celebration. In this way the sacramental sign, above all through its word, reveals its power to accomplish what it signifies. In the Eucharist the very sacrifice of Christ becomes present when the bread becomes the Body of Christ and the wine his Blood.

The Paschal mystery made present by the liturgy has the dynamism of the love of God, who has as his aim the salvation of every moment of human life. In the Liturgy of the Hours the various parts of the day are sanctified, so that, from the rising of the sun to its setting and in the heart of the night, the Church's thankful praise might rise to her Lord.

Liturgical space

With the multiplication of churches and images, the liturgy wishes to fill space with the memory of Christ the Savior and to make every place become a place for meeting God.

In this way conscience acquires the conviction that God is present in all places and that he is calling us to initiate a permanent dialogue with his gratuitous and faithful love. The liturgy unites us with Christ, from whom we learn to pray as children, and it sustains us in prayer with the strength of the Spirit, the Spirit of freedom and love, of trust and peace.

The *Catechism* teaches with clarity that the liturgy is not everything in the life of the Church, but it is for everything: it is the source of grace, because it contains the Paschal mystery; moreover, it is the summit toward which everything we do as pilgrims in search of the Father's house is directed (cf. *Sacrosanctum Concilium*, n. 10).

In the liturgy one encounters the most profound response in word and deed to the secularist mentality, since it offers Christ as the ultimate explanation of the meaning of creation and of the human person—all things were made "through him and for him" (Col 1: 16)—and, by recalling his plan, it makes present his redemptive action by means of which he draws to himself, heals and elevates individuals, peoples and cultures. The liturgy has a dynamism of its own which enables it to evangelize, or rather, to Christianize cultures.

This process, which is simply the extension of the mystery of the redemptive incarnation—Christ is the fullness of cultures—cannot come to an end except with history itself, because individuals and peoples always have the power to improve, and the Church the duty to redeem them in their new forms of life. This explains the diversity of liturgical traditions. The mystery of Pentecost is reflected in the plurality of rites in the one Catholic Church.

In an effort to express the catholicity of the faith, special care had to be taken during the drafting of the *Catechism* to assure that the Eastern tradition and that of the West were both kept in mind to an equal degree; in this way the text was enriched with the doctrine, piety and beauty of both. This purpose characterized the whole *Catechism*, but its influence is especially felt in the exposition of the sacramental economy. It is important to note the ecumenical value contained in this attitude with respect to our Orthodox brothers and sisters, who will find in the *Catechism* new proof of the respect and great love that Catholics have for every authentic Christian tradition.

Eschatological tension

The eschatological tension of hope is constantly and magnificently expressed in the liturgy, which is already a participation in time in the heavenly liturgy, and is wholly directed to heavenly glory. Its celebrations are none other than manifestations of the Paschal mystery of Christ, who begins his active reign through the sacraments and through the Church's entire apostolic activity, and promotes the final establishment of this kingdom in the *Parousia*. The eschatological dimension, so essential to the Christian mystery and so dear to Orientals and Protestants, was appropriately developed in the *Catechism*, especially in response to the fervent requests expressed at the beginning of the drafting process.

Hierarchy of truths

In the effort to respect the hierarchy of truths (cf. *Unitatis Redintegratio,* n. 11), that is, to relate the revealed mysteries to natural truths, to the other mysteries and to the final end (cf. Vatican I, DS 3016), an order was reached which shows the importance of the various truths in God's plan and contributes to their clarification. The very order of the parts of the *Catechism* is derived from the hierarchy of truths.

It must be said that the *leitmotiv* running throughout the *Catechism,* undergirding its unity and the sequence of exposition, is the truth of the Blessed Trinity, the mystery of mysteries, in its salvific economy; or in other words, the economy of the Trinity: the Father who sends his Son and his Spirit to save mankind in the Church. This principle determines the order:

- "the profession of faith" according to the Apostles' Creed and the Niceno-Constantinopolitan Creed;
- then, "the celebration of the Christian mystery", which is always the action of the divine Persons;
- thirdly the "life in Christ" in obedience to the Father and in the love of the Spirit;
- and finally, "Christian prayer", through which the children of God, conformed to the image of Christ through the work of the Holy Spirit, bless and worship the Father.

Conclusion

There are many other teachings of the *Catechism* on the liturgy. A thorough and devout study will be necessary in order to benefit from the riches of its defined truths and its serene, profound fervor.

If from Pope Paul VI we learned very clearly that the Church lives to evangelize (cf. *Evangelii Nuntiandi,* n. 14), under the inspiration of Vatican II and the *Catechism* we learn that the Church lives to celebrate, because the liturgy, and the Eucharist in a very special way, are the source and summit of evangelization and catechesis.

X

Catechism highlights centrality of sacraments in Christian life

by Jorge Medina Estévez
Bishop of Valparaíso, Chile

The 'sacramental' structure of salvation

The celebration of the sacraments is a central element in the life of the Church and, within the Church, of every disciple of Christ. A Church without sacraments would not be the Church of Christ for the simple reason that such a community would not be faithful to the concrete form of God's salvific plan in his Son, Jesus Christ.

Therefore, just as the Son of God took on human flesh in the most pure womb of the Virgin Mary and as Jesus Christ founded the Church to be a sign and instrument of his saving action at all times and places, in the same way the Lord Jesus himself established visible signs that are instruments through which and by which he made invisible grace present and operative in human beings.

In his human nature, Jesus Christ is the *sacrament of the Father;* the Church is the *sacrament of Christ* and each of her seven sacraments is an effective means of grace that, from the Father, through Christ, by the power of the Holy Spirit and through the ministry of the Church, reaches men and women to heal them and to *"divinize them"*, granting them the gift of future glory.

Thus the sacramental economy is rooted in the mystery of the incarnation. The merciful plan of the Father has decreed that salvation should come to human beings through the human nature of his Son: the *key* to the divine *strategy* lies in the fact that humanity is saved by means of a *bridge* reuniting it to God; This *bridge* will have a human nature, since in his *condescension* the Son of God would assume a true human nature so that the evil one may be defeated precisely where he claims victory. Jesus Christ saves us as Pontiff of the new covenant.

The first sin was caused by pride: the devil suggested to man and woman the fallacy of absolute autonomy "*You will be like gods!* . . ." (Gn 3: 5), as if human beings could rid themselves of their condition as creatures and, consequently, of the impelling need to live in a stance of adoration, the only way to live in truth.

Salvation then would necessarily have to come, so that man could rediscover the meaning of adoration and realize that life is meaningless unless it is lived in constant worship of God (cf. Rom 12: 1). Any human worship is therefore bound to include concrete expressions: matter, signs and words which tangibly express the deep reality of the invisible (cf. Heb 11: 3).

The sacraments of the Church

As a consequence we enter the world of these salvific realities, the seven sacraments of the Church.

Each of them is a *celebration,* a joyful experience of God's saving and sanctifying power. In each of them there is an essential agent, Jesus Christ, who communicates grace and salvation as the Pontiff of the new covenant. Every sacrament is celebrated in the Church, not only because the minister of the sacrament is the minister of Christ and of the Church, but also because sacramental celebration is a privileged moment of ecclesiality, a time when the community *"worships in spirit and in truth"* (cf. Jn 4: 23).

Hence the teaching of Vatican II, which declares that although "the sacred liturgy does not exhaust the entire activity of the Church, . . . nevertheless the liturgy is the summit toward which the activity of the Church is directed; it is also the fount from which all her power flows. For the goal of apostolic endeavor is that all who are made sons of God by faith and Baptism should come together to praise God in the midst of his Church, to take part in the Sacrifice and to eat the Lord's Supper . . .. From the liturgy therefore, and especially from the Eucharist, grace is poured forth upon us as from a fountain, and the sanctification of men in Christ and the glorification of God to which all other activities of the Church are directed, as towards their end, are achieved with maximum effectiveness" *(Sacrosanctum Concilium,* nn. 9-10).

It is therefore not a question of performing mere human rituals, which can be very expressive and beautiful but lacking in spiritual power, but of coming into contact with the mystery of Christ, with his saving work and also with the very person of Jesus Christ, through signs that bring grace, life in Christ and the promise of eternity.

The life of the Church has always been—and will always be—marked by the celebration of the sacraments. Proof of this in ancient times are the books of the New Testament and those venerable writings such as the *Didache,* the *Apologies* of St. Justin and the *Apostolic Tradition* of Hippolytus. These accounts already have a certain catechetical flavor.

Later the great Fathers of the Church would write more specifically catechetical works, generally starting from the basis of preparation for or celebration of Baptism: this is the case with St. Ambrose's explanations, contained in his works *De mysteriis* and *De sacramentis,* St. Augustine's noble work, *De catechizandibus rudibus* and the admirable catecheses of Jerusalem, works of the Bishops of that city, John or St. Cyril.

We cannot forget that the Creed develops around the baptismal liturgy and still has an important place in it today. It also belongs naturally to the Roman liturgy of the sacrament of Confirmation, and to that of the Sunday celebration of the Eucharist. Thus it can be seen how the profession of faith, the celebration of the sacraments, Christian life and the various forms of prayer are interpreted from different viewpoints.

Development of the doctrine on the sacraments

In many ancient Councils, both local and ecumenical, the Church continued to delineate and clarify her teaching on the sacraments, but not to the same degree, nor always on all the sacraments. However, a progressive development can be seen, emphasized in various acts of the Council of Florence (1439-1445), the conciliar Magisterium which was the immediate forerunner of the Council of Trent (1545-1563). Concerning the latter, it is enough to study its chapters and doctrinal canons to see that teaching about the sacraments has a very important place in it.

This can be understood not only as a reaction to the deviations and errors of the Protestant Reformation, but as something deeper: the need to strengthen a basic element of Catholic life and faith. As a logical consequence, the *Catechism of the Council of Trent* (published in 1566) contains in Part Two, the largest section, a detailed treatment of the sacraments.

Vatican II dealt with the sacraments in *Sacrosanctum Concilium* (nn. 36,47-82), *Lumen Gentium* (nn. 10,11,14,18-29,31,33,41), *Gaudium et Spes* (nn. 47-52), *Christus Dominus* (nn. 11 and 15), *Presbyterorum Ordinis* (nn. 5,7,13) and *Ad Gentes* (n. 14).

When Vatican II ended, during the pontificate of Pope Paul VI, the liturgy of the sacraments in use in the Latin Church was examined according to the directives provided by the Council, and the new rites of the sacraments and the new edition of the Roman Missal were published.

In the new rituals *(Ordines)* the rite itself is preceded by a liturgical introduction with valuable guidelines for the celebration of the sacrament itself and for its harmonious integration into the life of the Church, characterized throughout by a pastoral tone. These introductions are far more than mere "instructions" (precise indications on the correct way to carry out the liturgical rite): they are a true wellspring for liturgical ministry.

Although it is impossible to refer to all the recently published material from the Magisterium, it would be useful to recall the important decisions of Pope Pius XII on the sacrament of Orders (Apostolic Constitution *Sacramentum Ordinis,* of 30 November 1947; DS 3857-3861) and of Pope Paul VI regarding the sacraments of Baptism, Confirmation, Penance, the Anointing of the Sick and Orders (see the respective documents in the editions of the *Ordines* of the Roman Ritual).

The Code of Canon Law of the Latin Church promulgated in 1983 contains 325 canons on the sacraments, and the recently published Code of Canons of the Eastern Churches summarizes in 199 canons the common legislation on the sacraments for these Churches.

Sacramental doctrine in the '*Catechism of the Catholic Church*'

What has been said thus far serves as a basis for affirming that it is totally logical and consistent with Catholic tradition that the *Catechism* recently approved by Pope John Paul II should devote the whole of the Second Section of its Second Part to the seven sacraments of the Church. This section (nn. 1210-1666) comprises 16% of the whole *Catechism*. Taking into account the First Section of the Second Part, which contains the general doctrine on the liturgy, the amount dedicated to teaching about the celebration of the Christian mystery is 22% of the whole *Catechism*.

However, it is necessary to remember that the doctrine on the sacraments is deeply linked to the exposition of the faith, to the explanation of Christian morality and to teaching on prayer.

The *Catechism* should be read as a whole, since it is like a fabric in which some of its interwoven threads give meaning and solidity to others. No part of the *Catechism* is "*independent*" or able to be isolated from the other parts, and this is shown by the many cross-references.

Thus the Christian faith can be compared to a mosaic in which the colors and angles of light give a particular emphasis and vitality to the whole. This is one of the reasons why this book should not be read only once, but several times, in order gradually to perceive the inexhaustible richness of God's mystery and his saving love, as well as its notable organic unity.

Nothing can replace reading the text of the *Catechism* itself: its study will be a help for all those who exercise the ministry of proclaiming the Gospel and preaching the word of God. However, it would be helpful to emphasize certain aspects common to the exposition of sacramental doctrine in the *Catechism*. Among the most outstanding, the following four have been chosen.

Sacramental economy

The order in which the seven sacraments are treated is not arbitrary. St. Thomas Aquinas groups them into three "units":

- the three of Christian initiation, Baptism, Confirmation and the Eucharist;
- the two of care and healing, Penance and Anointing of the Sick;
- and finally, the two which are meant to structure the ecclesial community, Orders and Matrimony (cf. *Summa Theologiæ III, 65,1, c; 2 c*).

It would be mistaken to think that there are five "individual" and two "social" sacraments; each sacrament concerns the most intimate part of the person: his or her relationship with God, sanctification and the joy of giving glory to him; at the same time, each has a social dimension, a special ecclesial relationship to life in the visible Body of Christ, the Church.

In fact, Christian initiation is not merely an event that considers the person in an exclusively individual dimension: Baptism, Confirmation and the Eucharist introduce people into the Church, consolidate their membership in her, establish the apostolic and missionary spirit and confer unity in the faith through the gift of the Spirit and transformation in Christ. Penance not only heals Christians who are spiritually sick but, in granting them grace, also restores them to a normal situation within the Church. Anointing of the Sick, comforting them in physical pain, associates them with the mystery of salvation that is fulfilled and lived in the Church.

From another perspective, Orders and Matrimony not only have a social and community aspect, but are also sources of personal grace and holiness for Christians who are called by God to live in the state of ministry to the Church or as Christian spouses.

Thus in the Church "the personal" is lived in the mysterious communion of the Body of Christ, and the "social" has no truly Christian dimension if it does not maintain a deep and radical relationship with grace and holiness in view of the ultimate personal vocation of the human being, which is glory.

It is necessary to keep in mind that Scripture describes the glorious happiness of eternal life with a series of community images: the "Father's house", the "banquet of the kingdom", "the heavenly Jerusalem".

Biblical dimension

Vatican II devoted one of its Dogmatic Constitutions, *Dei Verbum*, to the topic of the word of God, and specifically, to that of Sacred Scripture. The Christian faith shows that the biblical writings were inspired by God and that through them we come to know divine revelation and the facts and words by which God communicates with us for the purpose of our salvation. This is why Scripture has an irreplaceable role in the life of the Church.

It is enough to consider the important place a pulpit occupies in a house of worship, the place from which the biblical readings are proclaimed, in order to understand that the Scriptures are not a food reserved for "scholars" or a group of the elite but are the bread that comes from the mouth of God, giving life to the human person (cf. Mt 4: 4), to all those who accept the Word who dwells among us (cf. Jn 1: 10-14).

For this reason there is nothing strange about the fact that the Bishops in charge of drafting the *Catechism* asked that it be based mainly on Scripture and that the doctrine be elaborated with frequent references to biblical texts, read and considered in the context of the great Tradition of the Church whose witnesses are the Fathers and saints of all time.

The biblical texts that appear in the *Catechism* are not mere *dicta probantia*, but have been chosen with a view to help explain a specific doctrine's relationship to the whole of the mystery, i.e., God's plan of salvation for humanity. The Bible will therefore be the book that should always be in the hands of those who are reading the *Catechism*. It would be a great impoverishment to see the *Catechism* as a "substitute" for the Scriptures. It serves Scripture, just as it also serves Catholic Tradition and the authentic Magisterium.

In the summary texts found at the end of the teaching on each of the sacraments, a biblical text related to the institution of the respective sacrament has been added. These texts should be read in the light of Tradition and the Magisterium, since this alone is the basis for the certitude of faith that the Church and the believer have regarding their nature and the saving purpose that Jesus Christ assigned to each of the sacred grace-bearing signs (cf. *Dei Verbum,* n. 9).

The mystagogic dimension

According to St. Thomas Aquinas, the sacraments belong to the "family" of signs *(Summa Theologiæ,* III, q. 60, a. 1; c.; a. 4, c., *ad 1).* They are "visible forms of invisible grace" (ibid., III, q. 60, a. 2, c.; Council of Trent, DS 1606, 1607, 1639) and for this reason, in explaining the sacraments' meaning and effect, the Church Fathers often took the liturgical celebration as their starting point and paused to comment on each of the elements of the sacramental rite. Through these signs the faithful perceived the rich doctrine of the effects of each sacrament, that is, its special grace or salvific effect that constitutes at the same time its purpose and its result.

The *Catechism of the Catholic Church* has endeavored to emphasize the mystagogic method in explaining the sacraments, inviting Pastors and faithful to penetrate their spiritual meaning through the signs of the liturgical celebration. Dealing with the doctrine on each sacrament, the *Catechism* has summarized as precisely as possible the special effect of grace belonging to each.

Thus the multiple richness of the Holy Spirit's action upon the children of the Church is brought out, and one sees how true and valid are St. Paul's words at every moment of Christian life: "We live for the Lord" (Rom 14: 8).

The ecclesial dimension

It is traditional to speak of the "sacraments of the Church". They do not belong to the Church because she has instituted them, nor because she is the origin of grace, nor because she may dispose of them as she sees fit. The Church "administers" them on behalf of Jesus Christ and in conformity with his mandate. They are therefore "of" the Church because:

- Jesus Christ entrusted them to her to be "administered" faithfully, in conformity with the mandate of her Spouse and Lord;
- they constitute the culminating acts of the presence of saving grace;
- they are the apex of her activity and service;
- through them the Christian community that the Church serves not only expresses itself, but also grows in grace and holiness;
- legitimate participation in the sacraments is an expression and bond of communion.

The Church cannot act arbitrarily in giving or refusing the sacraments: it is a right of the faithful that Pastors give them the sacraments, and the Pastors have a corresponding duty (cf. *Lumen Gentium*, n. 37; CIC, can. 213-843). This is why it is correct to say that the Church is a servant of the sacraments: her mission is to communicate them so that God's children "may have life and have it to the full" (Jn 10: 10). To be a servant does not mean that this task implies no responsibility: the sacraments are not administered as if they were some sort of material possession, but on the condition that they are received with the dispositions that allow them "to bear fruit, fruit that will last" (Jn 15: 16; CIC, can. 843, 2). Thus the Church should ensure the proper preparation of those who ask for the sacraments and establish the pastoral norms that truly encourage their fruitful reception.

Conclusion

All the sacraments draw their strength and effectiveness from Christ's Paschal mystery : all grace springs from the re-deeming sacrifice of the cross and the power of the victorious Christ, the risen Christ. Every time the Church celebrates the sacramental signs, she renders the work of salvation present and effective. This work is called to permeate the whole of human existence: to purify it, to enlighten it, to strengthen it, to sustain it, to integrate it, to make it whole and to direct it towards eternity. This work can be known only through revelation and faith, it is made present with maximum effect in the sacramental liturgy, assumes a concrete form in Christian existence lived in conformity with the Gospel, and is the basic "theme" of prayer in the Church, the privileged expression of the "praise and glory of the grace" of God and his plan of salvation (cf. Eph 1: 6-12,14).

XI

Catechism presents morality as a lived experience of faith in Christ

by Jean Honoré
Archbishop of Tours, France

Like the other three parts of the *Catechism of the Catholic Church,* the part dedicated to the moral life of the Christian has two sections:

- the first, an extensive introduction, lays the foundations for this moral life, defines its orientations and explains its spirit;

- the second treats each commandment of the Decalogue in turn and explains its proper observance and place in the dynamism of perfection that is contained in the Gospel call to follow Christ.

The long introduction to the presentation of the Ten Commandments is precisely what constitutes the new Catechism's originality compared with the *Catechismus ad Parochos,* resulting from the Council of Trent, whose moral section opens with the study of the first commandment. It is also the introduction which gives balance to this section of the *Catechism,* in comparison to the others, in particular the first that presents the creed, and the second, that relates to the liturgy and the sacraments. But this harmony of parts reflected in the final version of the *Catechism* was only reached after successive drafts, each of which required a patient effort of reflection and sometimes laborious debate.

Right from the start of the undertaking, the two Bishops who were entrusted with the moral section had continually to deli-

berate on what perspective and framework to give to the introduction that would eventually become *Section I of the Third Part
of the Catechism.* In more technical terms, it was mainly a question
of drawing the outlines of what is called *morality in general,*
distinguishing it from *specific moral questions* which are developed in the commandments and the precepts of the Decalogue.

For a coherent, organic whole

Without a doubt, from the beginning there was a certain idea of
what needed to be done. After the first two parts of the *Catechism,*
which in their development *focused on the faith*—its transmission
in the first and its celebration in the second—there could be no
question of deviating from it in the third. It was essential to keep
this *reference* to faith, which was meant to unify the whole work.
It was therefore the *faith testified to* through the fulfillment of the
vocation of the baptized that was to be the basis for the drafts and
to give unity to the section on morals.

But while we were quite aware of the project's scope, we were less
sure of how to arrange the many elements pertaining to morality.

Traditionally, moral thought gravitates around several themes:

- some are of an *anthropological* nature (conscience, freedom
  and responsibility, solidarity . . .);

- others are of an *ethical and normative nature* (the law, its
  various levels and the different stages of transmission . . .);

- finally, there is the more *specific* theme of qualifying human
  actions according to whether they are an expression of the
  practice of virtue or derive from sin.

All these ideas, knowledge of which is indispensable for *evaluat-
ing* moral conduct, had first to be mastered and summarized in a
coherent and organic presentation.

Several problems familiar to theologians were bound to arise.

Here are a few examples:

How to present the relationship between the law, an *objective*
standard of morality, and the *subjective* conscience of the individual in deciding his actions? How to establish the connection

between natural law and divine law, reconciling the prescriptions of the Decalogue and the new commandment of the Gospels, which sums them all up, since according to St. Paul *"love is the bond of perfection"* (Col 3: 14)?

Was the Decalogue to be held up as a universal framework for morality, or, as a number of Bishops were soon to request, should the exposition of morality follow another plan, such as the one provided by reference to the Beatitudes or to the theological and moral virtues, as St. Thomas had done in his *Summa Theologiæ?* Choices had inevitably to be made between the different editorial options.

At this point, it might be fitting to pay Cardinal Ratzinger the tribute that is due him for the wisdom, the intellectual rigor and the courtesy with which he directed the debates and guided the drafting of the texts!

Spiritual dynamism

The most important dimension is yet to be mentioned. The editorial parameters not only had to respect all aspects of the ethical themes, but also their natural sequence, as mentioned above. Each of these themes had to be inserted into a text which, in addition to being coherent, aimed at presenting a truly dynamic vision of morality, with its appeals and especially with the spirit inspiring them and running through all its chapters.

As well as ensuring the accuracy of its ethical statements, was it not necessary to give these texts a certain inner life? They were to create an awareness of the way to conversion and moral progress, using many quotations from the Fathers of the Church and many examples from the lives of the saints to demonstrate their value and attraction.

We were aware of the pitfall to be avoided: presenting and describing Christian life in terms of a code of morality, as a treatise of good behavior, as though all that mattered was to learn to judge, label, punish or soothe consciences faced with the demands and trials of living moral lives. At all costs it was imperative to avoid the danger of casuistry and to give ultimate meaning and motivation to the moral life of Christians. This ultimate sense could only be the one radiating from the Beatitudes, and the motivation none other than that of the *sequela Christi* (following Christ), a *sequela Christi* seen not only as the imitation of a model viewed from the outside, but as a true *identification* with Christ's inner being, consisting entirely in a relationship and submission to the Father, and in the perfection of witnessing by a life belonging entirely to him.

In fact, this is the heart of the insight that was to introduce and give unity to the chapter on morality: the faith of the disciple, expressed in the Creed, celebrated in the sacraments, is revealed in the witness of life and the response given to the Gospel's call to perfection. This general thematic arrangement of Section I received its first finishing touches in the version referred to as the "revised draft" that was submitted to the Bishops for consultation in October 1989.

Agreement and disagreement . . .

This is not the place to recall the criticisms and proposed amendments (*modi*) voiced in the universal consultation of the Bishops. The section on morals was discussed particularly, despite a generally favorable view of its modern approach. In a later article in this series criticisms relating to the presentation of certain precepts of the Decalogue will be discussed.

As for the First Section , the major criticisms were the following:

- First of all, its length, 30 pages was considered too short in comparison with other parts such as doctrine and liturgy. It was deemed necessary to develop further certain subjects, and even to include others.

- The second criticism, as we have seen, concerned the choice of keeping to the framework of the Decalogue, while reference to the Beatitudes and to the virtues had seemed more positive and more evangelical.

No matter what option was taken, the chapter on the virtues was too short and needed to be rewritten.

In the eyes of many Bishops, this First Part of the Catechism's section on morality was so totally focused on the anthropology of the individual that it tended to ignore *the social and community dimension* of human beings. It was therefore decided to draft a new chapter that would in fact make it possible to combine certain moral precepts of the commandments, particularly the seventh, and thus lighten the text. The whole of the second chapter of Section I recalls this aspect of the human condition and presents the duties of solidarity within the different communities where each person's destiny is fulfilled.

Beyond moralism

A final criticism concerned a question which had already arisen among those in charge of drafting the *Catechism*. To use Kantian language, however categorical the imperative of a moral life motivated by the Gospel call to follow Christ may be, however many references from the Scriptures and from the earliest tradition of the Fathers prevented one from likening the moral life of believers to mere virtuous conformity, the draft of the *Catechism* at that stage still gave rise to a radical and undeniably well-founded criticism.

Indeed, while the *Catechism* succeeded in expressing the call to follow the Gospel and aim at perfection, it did not show (or at least not sufficiently) that this quest can only be accomplished by the baptized with the help of the gratuitous grace that heals and absolves them from sin and supports them along the way. In brief, because it had not been stated fully or with sufficient clarity, it was not immediately obvious that whatever Christians do in the order of salvation and holiness, they do not *do alone, but only with divine assistance.* In their effort to grow in virtue, all Christians, even the greatest saints, are justified and saved sinners.

By failing to emphasize the prevenient action of the Lord's grace and the inner presence of the Spirit, the *Catechism* was in danger of omitting one of the most basic conditions of moral action according to the Gospel. A conscious effort had been made to avoid the trap of casuistry. That of moralism was narrowly avoided. The draft could be said to have retained a Pelagian tone that still had to be corrected.

To tell the truth, the first editors were not unaware of this problem. They had considered which part of the *Catechism* was most suitable for the doctrine of justification. Some suggested the end of the chapter in Part I on the Redemption by Christ. Preference was given to the section on morality, and rightly so, for it is precisely the essay on *grace and justification* (Chapter III, art. 2) that gives perfect balance to the doctrinal synthesis of this whole First Section that develops the Christian vocation as life in the Spirit. The logic of the three chapters can clearly be seen:

- the person considered in his dignity as image of God and in his vocation;
- the person considered as a social being with his ties of solidarity;
- finally, God's initiative as expressed in the twofold gift he makes to man with a view to his vocation: law and grace.

It was therefore this plan that, at each new stage in the drafting and the subsequent debates, was finally adopted. These divisions and the framework of the *Catechism* are clear in the form in which it is now being offered to the faithful.

By learning to recognize them, the faithful discover the perspectives and measure the real challenge of the norms and prescriptions of moral life. For the baptized, morality has no other meaning than to seek to identify one's life with *"life in Christ"*, the expression so dear to the Apostle Paul which has given its title to the whole of Part III of the *Catechism*.

The primacy given to following Christ, to docility to the Holy Spirit, to the requirement of perfection that is at the same time a response to divine grace and the breakthrough of the Gospel, gives theological depth to the teaching on morals. It is revealed less as a collection of precepts made in the name of a law, than as the *ever renewed response to an ever recurring call*. In fact, if we have to speak of moral life in terms of obedience, let us speak less of obedience to the law than of the *obedience of faith* (cf. Rom 1: 5).

XII

The Ten Commandments provide a positive framework for life in Christ

David Every Konstant
Bishop of Leeds, England

In Part III of the *Catechism*, "The faith lived", the Ten Commandments form the framework for Catholic moral teaching. This was
obviously not an inescapable choice. The Creed, an ancient,
solemn and universal form of Christian profession, is plainly the
best setting for doctrinal teaching. The sacraments clearly mark
the shape of the faith as it is celebrated. But the Decalogue is an
Old Testament form whose relation to the Gospel and to the
Christian ideal of holiness is not so immediately plain. Some
formulations of Christian morality have used the virtues as their
framework. It has been suggested that the Beatitudes might in
some way provide its most distinctive shape and character. What
is it then about the Decalogue which makes it the best framework
for moral teaching and moral life?

First, when we reflect on the witness of the Holy Scriptures,
it is plain that these "ten words" are the word of God in a
privileged sense beyond the other laws written by Moses.
They are given on the holy mountain, they are "inscribed by
the finger of God" (Ex 31: 28). This gift takes place in the
context of the Exodus, the great liberating event which
formed the center of the old covenant. Whether their form is
negative ("You shall not kill") or positive ("Honor your father
and your mother"), they make plain the character and quality
of a life which is freed from enslavement to sin.

The "ten words" are spoken during a theophany and they form part of God's self-revelation. "On the mountain from the heart of the fire, Yahweh spoke to you face to face" (Dt 5: 4). This revelation establishes the covenant, a close and faithful alliance between God and his people. The Ten Commandments find their true meaning at the heart of this covenant. They make explicit the nature and the demands of this loving relationship. Hence they transform and illuminate moral life. It is more than correct behavior, more than rational rules or social discipline. It is in essence a response to God's gift of himself. Moral life is suffused with the spirit of glad homage to God and of thanksgiving.

The central importance of the Decalogue is underlined by the words of the Gospel in which Jesus sustained, reaffirmed, fulfilled and perfected it. "If you wish to enter into life", he said, "keep the commandments". And he went on to specify: "You must not kill. You must not commit adultery. You must not bring false witness. Honor your father and your mother." Finally he summarized these commandments in a positive tone, "You must love your neighbor as yourself" (Mt 19: 1-19).

Christians have given central importance to Ten Commandments

A second reply followed: "If you wish to be perfect, go and sell what you own and give the money to the poor . . . then, come, follow me" (Mt 19: 21). The old law is not abolished. The young man in the Gospel is called first to observe it and secondly to go beyond it in discipleship, following the way of the Master in whom the moral perfection of holiness is fully embodied. The evangelical counsels rest upon the commandments and grow out of them. Jesus preaches a justice which goes deeper than that of the scribes and Pharisees (Mt 5: 20), which expands but does not annul their justice. The twofold commandment of love provides the two foundations on which the Ten Commandments rest, the two sources from which they derive their true meaning and their value.

Following the Lord's lead, Christian tradition has given to the Ten Commandments a place of central importance as it expressed and detailed its moral teaching. At least since the time of St. Augustine, the Decalogue has maintained a prominent place in the structure and content of catechesis. Over the centuries, many of the Church's catechisms have shaped their moral teaching according to the order of the commandments, the first three articulating our duty to God, the other seven our obligation to our neighbors. Thus they have become hallowed by tradition.

Thus Christian moral experience and moral teaching have accumulated within the setting of the Decalogue, and have there discovered their true selves and their deepest meaning. Within that setting even the complex, rapidly changing problems of late 20th-century life can best find their moral bearing.

The Ten Commandments are part of God's revelation. They also disclose to us our true humanity. In bringing to light essential human obligations, they also create the foundations of basic human rights. Thus they are a reinforcement and a powerful re-expression of the natural law. The relevance of the Ten Commandments goes beyond the boundaries of salvation history and Christian tradition. They form a privileged part of the moral thought and discourse of mankind.

"From the beginning", wrote St. Irenæus (Adv. *Hær.* 4: 51,1), "God rooted the principles of the natural law in the human heart. It was enough for him to recall them. This he did in the Decalogue." We know God's commandments through God's revelation as it comes to us in the heart of the Church. They echo in our own hearts where the voice of conscience speaks.

The Decalogue, then, is not a rigid, inflexible framework into which moral questions and teachings have to be awkwardly crammed without fitting very well. Rather, woven into salvation history, confirmed and perfected by the Gospel, cherished and articulated in the Church's life, it constitutes an organic tradition of moral wisdom like the tradition within which doctrine develops, a tradition at the service of faith which can assimilate and order new moral experiences and dilemmas when these arise.

It may be said that to give the commandments so prominent a place in Christian moral teaching will create about that teaching a negative atmosphere. We have seen already that not all the commandments have the negative form, "You shall not . . ."; some command us to act, not to abstain. Moreover, the purpose of the commandments in general, as they come to us, is not to restrict freedom but to open the way to a truly liberated life. To do this it is necessary to mark off those ways which lead by the route of illusory satisfactions, to falsity and death. "There are two ways, the one leading to life, the other to death, and between the two there is a great difference" *(Didache* 1: 1).

The commandments do not stand in splendid isolation, like the pillars of principle on which all the rest of morality depends. As a framework for moral catechesis they provide the structure for a rich fabric into which other themes are woven. We must point to these in order to disclose the joys as well as the cost of the way of Christ.

A catechesis of *the Holy Spirit* reveals the presence of an interior guide moving among the roots of our choices: a strengthening spirit who inspires and guides the true life and sets it to rights.

Grace of Christ enables us to grow in holiness

The theme of *grace* points to the fortifying truth that moral life is not a solitary struggle of the will. That grace of Christ which saves us continues to work in our hearts, enabling us to grow towards fruitful holiness. "Whoever remains in me, with me in him, bears fruit in plenty; for cut off from me you can do nothing" (Jn 15: 5).

The catechesis of the *Beatitudes* raises moral life into the structure of God's kingdom; that of the human and Christian *virtues* shows the attraction of goodness and the beauty of holiness; that of the *twofold commandment of charity* opens our eyes to the true root of moral life, to the reality of love. The truths of *sin* and *forgiveness* are also a necessary theme. If we do not recognize ourselves to be sinners we do not truly know ourselves. Self-knowledge is the condition for right action. But only the unfailing offer of forgiveness makes it bearable; makes it, though bitter, a source of humility, faith and salvation.

Finally a catechesis of the *Church* places moral life within a life-giving community of faith. Within the "communion of the saints" moral understanding and the life of grace can grow and can communicate itself to the world.

The Decalogue comes to us as a privileged reality in our heritage of faith and an indispensable structure and source of moral and spiritual life. Hence, wrote the Fathers of the Second Vatican Council, "the Bishops, successors of the Apostles, receive from the Lord the mission to teach all nations and to preach the Gospel to all; so that everyone through faith, through Baptism and through fulfilling the commandments may come to salvation" *(Lumen Gentium, n. 24).*

XIII

In the name of Jesus we have confident access to the Father

by Fr. Jean Corbon
International Theological Commission

In order to awaken and nourish the understanding of the faith, the fourth part of the *Catechism*, even more than the others, demands a prayerful reading: "One does not learn to see; it is an effect of nature. The beauty of prayer is also something that cannot be learned by the teaching of another. It has its master in itself, God who gives prayer to the one who prays" (St. John Climacus, *Degree* 28; *PG 88*, 1130).

This is why the original draft of the *Catechism* placed as an epilogue the prayer *par excellence* which we received from the Lord: the "Our Father". But at the end of the Bishops' consultation on the revised draft (1989-1990), the majority of the responses asked to have the presentation of the "Our Father" preceded by an exposition on Christian prayer. And this is how the First Section of Part IV came about.

The nuance of its title should be noted: "Prayer *in* the Christian life". In this way the meaning of Christian prayer is emphasized, not as one occupation among many others, but as a "living and personal relationship with the living and true God" (n. 2558) at the heart of our life in Christ. In the doctrinal presentation that the Church offers us in this *Catechism*, prayer appears as the summit because it is founded on faith (Part I), is strengthened by the sacraments of faith (Part II) and is active in charity (Part III); but *in* our daily lives it is primary, because it is that "enthusiasm of the heart" (n. 2558) through which the Holy Spirit, who is our life, makes us act as well (cf. Gal 5: 25). Prayer is thus, in our lives, both the fruit and the lifeblood of the mystery of salvation proclaimed throughout the *Catechism.*

Our prayer is *Christian,* that is to say through Christ, with him and in him. The beauty of this divine/human mystery of Christian prayer is apparent from the beginning of this section (nn. 2559-2565): as a gift of God and a human response, as the "new covenant" in Christ lived in the human heart, as communion with the Father and his Son, Jesus Christ, in the Holy Spirit, a communion *(koinonia)* which expands in the Church and whose dimensions are those of the love of Christ (cf. Eph 3: 18, 21).

But how can the Church teach the children of God to pray to the Father with Christ in the Holy Spirit? From the earliest ages, the Fathers of the Church, saints and spiritual masters have written treatises on prayer, each according to the mentality and needs of his readers.

The present *Catechism,* leaving to the Bishops and their catechists the task of its inculturation, has simply followed the logic of salvation history, that long journey of God with man, so that man may respond to his God, accept his covenant and finally live in fellowship with him. Hence this section is divided into three chapters: the revelation of prayer, the tradition of prayer, the life of prayer.

The revelation of prayer is identical with "the words and actions" of the economy of salvation *(Dei Verbum,* n. 2); it goes from the beginning of time to "the fullness of time" and up to the beginning of the first Christian communities. From here, "it is by a living transmission (sacred Tradition) that the Holy Spirit, in the 'believing and praying Church' *(Dei Verbum,* n. 8), teaches the children of God to pray" (n. 2650). This is how Christian prayer enters into our lives and becomes "the life of the new heart" (n. 2697).

The revelation of prayer and the universal call to prayer

The subtitle of this chapter attracts our attention. "Man is in search of God . . .. All religions testify to this fundamental quest of human beings." But, and this is the novelty of Revelation, it is "God who first calls man . . .. As God gradually reveals himself and reveals man to himself, prayer appears as a mutual call, a covenant event . . .. Prayer is linked to the history of human beings, it is the relationship to God in the events of history . . . beginning with the realities of creation." Throughout the first nine chapters of Genesis appear the first signs of this human prayer, "lived by a multitude of the just in all religions . . . (for) in his unbreakable covenant with living beings God is always calling people to prayer" (nn. 2566-2569). The importance of these paragraphs will not escape those who are engaged in interreligious dialogue. The "universal" prayer of the faithful will also find here a new expansiveness of love.

From our father Abraham to the coming of the Savior, the sacred books of the Old Testament reveal to us the genesis of Christian prayer through the saving events and, in each stage, through the great giants of prayer who are its prophets:

- the promise and the prayer of faith;
- Moses and the prayer of the mediator;
- David and the prayer of the king;
- Elijah, the prophets and conversion of heart;
- and that inexhaustible treasure, the psalms, the prayer of the assembly (nn. 2570-2589).

This re-reading of the Scriptures to "search" for the one to whom they bear witness (cf. Jn 5: 39) is always relevant: the same Holy Spirit, who taught our ancestors in the faith how to pray by participating in the divine plan of salvation, guides us according to the same pedagogy along the only way, Christ.

The article which follows (In the fullness of time, nn. 2598-2619) is at the center of the First Section: "Here the novelty of (Christian) prayer begins to be revealed: *filial prayer,* which the Father awaited from his children, was finally to be lived by the only Son himself in his humanity, with and for human beings" (n. 2599).

Jesus prays, Jesus teaches to pray, Jesus answers prayer: in him the Holy Spirit tells us everything we need to know about

Christian prayer. These rich passages cannot be summarized; they plunge us into the heart of the Gospel. One cannot read them without being drawn into the prayer of the Lord Jesus. The prayer of the Virgin Mary (nn. 2617-2619) embraces the fullness of the time of salvation with silence, faith and intercession, from the annunciation to Jesus' hour and to Pentecost. Her canticle of thanksgiving will become that of the Church.

In the age of the Church, beginning with Pentecost, the revelation of prayer concerns the communal and personal forms of prayer which are still normative for Christian prayer: blessing and adoration, petition (especially for forgiveness), intercession, thanksgiving and praise (nn. 2623-2643). "The Eucharist contains and expresses all the forms of prayer: it is 'the pure offering' of the whole Body of Christ." This is why it remains the home of the living tradition of Christian prayer.

The tradition of prayer

"The tradition of Christian prayer is one of the ways in which the tradition of faith grows, particularly through the contemplation and study of believers who ponder in their hearts the events and words of the economy of salvation, and from the intimate sense of spiritual realities which they experience" (n. 2651, citing *Dei Verbum,* n. 8).

"The Holy Spirit is the 'living water' which, in the praying heart, 'springs up to eternal life' (Jn 4: 14). It is he who teaches us to draw from the Source itself: Christ. Now there are in Christian life certain springs where Christ awaits us in order to give us to drink of the Holy Spirit": the word of God (the Spirit makes us know Christ), the Church's liturgy (the Spirit actualizes the saving event), the theological virtues (through our minds the Spirit puts us into communion with the Father and the Son), finally the "today" of God (in daily events the Spirit brings us into harmony with the will of Christ wholly given over to the Father) (nn. 2652-2660).

The apostolic Tradition reminds us of the Way to the living sources of prayer: "The sacred humanity of Jesus is the way by which the Holy Spirit teaches us to pray to God our Father." It is "in the name of Jesus" that we have filial and confident access to the Father.

A series of three elements gives us a modest outline of this way:

- prayer to the Father,
- prayer to Jesus,
- "Come, Holy Spirit" (nn. 2664-2672).

But the holy Mother of God "shows us the Way" *(Hodegetria)*, as a transparent sign of the one Mediator (nn. 2673-2679). It is easy to see why in these pages devoted to the way of prayer, and in those which follow (guides for prayer, nn. 2683-2691), the *Catechism* is briefer and limits itself to what is basically common to all the Churches.

In fact, in the living tradition of prayer, it is "each Church which offers the language of prayer to her faithful, according to the historical, social and cultural context: words, melodies, gestures, iconography. It pertains to the Magisterium to discern the fidelity of these paths of prayer to the tradition of the apostolic faith, and it pertains to the Pastors and catechists to explain their meaning, always with reference to Jesus Christ" (n. 2663).

The life of prayer

This same concern to respect the particular traditions of the Churches explains the simplicity, but also the richness of this last chapter. We are here in the realm of the spiritual experience of the child of God "face to face" with his God. This is why, both in the expressions of personal prayer (vocal prayer, meditation, mental prayer) and in the struggle of prayer (objections, difficulties, fundamental dispositions), the *Catechism* does not adopt any one school of spirituality, but rather develops biblical spirituality in the light of the common experience of the spiritual writers of East and West (nn. 2697-2745).

Jesus' priestly prayer (cf. Jn 17) contains the whole mystery of Christian prayer. "It remains always his own, just as his Passover, having taken place 'once for all', remains present in the liturgy of his Church." "It embraces the whole economy of creation and salvation." "It is by entering into the holy name of the Lord Jesus that we are able to receive, from within, the prayer which he teaches us: 'Our Father' " (nn. 2746 2751).

As will be seen in the Second Section, the priestly prayer of Jesus inspires the great petitions of the Lord's Prayer. The above brief analysis of this text on "Prayer in the Christian life" did not allow us to dwell at each stage on the great currents which inspired it. Let it suffice to mention them now:

• The grace of the kingdom is "the union of the whole Blessed Trinity with the whole mind" (St. Gregory Nazianzen) (n. 2565).

• "The life of prayer is to be habitually in the presence of the thrice-holy God and in communion with him" (n. 2665).

• Christian prayer is that of Christ, our Head, in which we participate as his members. It is "filial".

• Christian prayer participates in the history of salvation which is an event of the covenant between God and all human beings. Through words and actions, this theme engages the heart, the place of covenant, the place of prayer.

• Christian prayer participates in the divine concern for the salvation of all. "Yes, Father!" The loving will of the Father fills the heart which prays.

• Christian prayer is prayer "in the Church" for the life of the world.

• Christian prayer springs from thanksgiving and, even in petition, is borne aloft by adoration and praise.

XIV

'Our Father' offers the Christian a complete synthesis of prayer

J. Castellano Cervera, O.C.D.
*Consultant to the Congregation
for the Doctrine of the Faith*

The Church received from the Lord the gift of prayer and the task of teaching how to pray. When Jesus, revealing himself as both model and teacher of prayer, replied to his disciples' request: "Teach us to pray!" (cf. Lk 11: 1), he gave the Church the Lord's Prayer, saying: "When you pray say: 'Father'" (ibid., 2). The Lord's prayer in the Gospel of Luke precedes a developed catechesis on prayer, while in the Gospel of Matthew it is placed within the context of the Sermon on the Mount, among the teachings on authentic prayer (cf. Mt 6: 9-13). By teaching the "Our Father" to his disciples, Jesus gave them a formula that was brief but rich in content for faith and life; the key to understanding it is in the main word: "Father". It reveals the mystery of God as Father and the dignity of Christians as children, and therefore brothers and sisters.

The Lord's Prayer, in fact, expresses succinctly the essential wealth of the new filial relationship with the Father which the beloved Son came to reveal to us, the fraternal communion of all, the fundamental unity of the prayer and actions of the Lord's disciples, the opening to grace and to the hope that is at the basis of the Christian vocation, and the trust in God's promises and gifts of which we are in constant need and which we must implore through prayer. By giving the disciples the "prayer of the kingdom", the Lord enabled his Church, by the grace of the

Holy Spirit, to transmit to all generations the gift of prayer, its most original formula, and the catechesis necessary for learning to pray.

In her *Catechism* the Catholic Church, faithful to the gift received from the divine Master, offers the people of our day, who are clearly seeking an authentic relationship with God, a fundamental catechesis on the *Pater Noster,* almost as a compendium and a living support of the faith that is professed, of the mystery of Christ which is celebrated, of the commitment to lead a new life, a true synthesis of Christian prayer itself. In this way the explanation of the Lord's Prayer acts rather as the conclusion and the seal of the whole *Catechism of the Catholic Church.*

Lord's Prayer renews baptismal awareness

By offering the Lord's Prayer as the summary of Christian prayer, the Church does not take the place of her Lord and Master but hands on today, as she has always done, a clear synthesis of the teaching of the Gospel words and once again offers the people of our time the perennial, unchanged and unsurpassable prayer of the divine Master.

As the Christians' own prayer, the "Our Father" belongs to the "deposit of faith", transmitted by Scripture and Tradition. From the very first days of the Church's existence, it began to form part of the faith professed and lived. As the *Didaché* testifies, the early Christian communities recited it three times a day, almost as if it were their daily profession of faith. Its explanation was perceived as the essential "initiation" into the faith and life of new Christians. As early as the fourth century, as we see from the baptismal catecheses, the Lord's Prayer was taught and explained in its deepest meaning to catechumens and neophytes before and after Baptism. Its official consignment during the catechumenate marked the moment of the *traditio orationis dominicæ,* as Augustine says, and it was preceded by an extensive catechesis preparing for the celebration of Baptism, when for the first time the neophytes could call God "Father" with full right and confidence, thus being united with the community of the faithful. Even today in the *Rite of Christian Initiation of Adults,* the rite of the "consignment" *(traditio)* of the Lord's Prayer by the Church and of the later "reconsignment" (*redditio*) by the "illuminandi", forms part of the baptismal journey and supposes a catechesis and a profound study of the meaning and content of that prayer that Christians "dare to say", especially during the Eucharistic celebration. It renews in us our baptismal consciousness, in such a way that in a sermon attributed to St. Augustine, the proclamation of the Lord's Prayer is described as "our daily Baptism."

The Church's Tradition, by the light of the Holy Spirit, has discovered unfathomable riches of faith and life in the words of the Lord. In the Lord's Prayer, Augustine saw the climax and the summation of all the prayer of the Old Testament, especially of the psalms. Tertullian presented it as "the synthesis of the whole Gospel". St. Thomas defines it as the "most perfect prayer". For St. Teresa of Jesus, the Lord's Prayer contains "the whole way of the spiritual life".

From Christian Tradition we have inherited commentaries of great theological, spiritual and catechetical worth. Tertullian and Origen offered us the first fruits of spiritual exegesis in their treatises on prayer. In his *De oratione dominica* St. Cyprian gave us the first commentary expressly devoted to the Lord's Prayer. Cyril of Jerusalem and Theodore of Mopsuestia in the East, and Ambrose and Augustine in the West, inserted into the catechesis on Baptism and the Eucharist a brief explanation of each word of the Lord's Prayer. Many are the commentaries of the Fathers on Matthew's and Luke's versions found in the patristic literature of East and West.

The Lord's Prayer also had its poetic versions in ancient authors, such as in a hymn of Ambrose and especially in the *Carmen paschale* of Sedulius. Dante too inserted a poetic elaboration of it in his *Divine Comedy*. The theological commentary of St. Thomas is famous as is the spiritual commentary of St. Teresa of Jesus in her *Way of Perfection*, to cite but a few of the most famous commentaries. In modern times the explanation of the Lord's Prayer forms part of the great catechisms, from the *Catechismus maior* of St. Peter Canisius to the *Roman Catechism* of St. Pius V.

'Our Father' has a Trinitarian dimension

In the wake of the *Roman Catechism* and in line with Tradition, the *Catechism of the Catholic Church* gives a careful catechetical synthesis of the Lord's Prayer and offers us a concrete, essential and appropriate commentary for today's believer. After a short explanation of the setting in which Jesus teaches the Lord's Prayer in the Gospels of Luke and Matthew, the *Catechism* proposes Matthew's formula, which is the one used by the Church, and adds to it a note on the final doxology: "For the kingdom, the power and the glory are yours, now and forever" (nn. 2959-2960).

This is an addition testified to with some variations from the *Didache* and the *Apostolic Constitutions* and preserved in the Byzantine tradition. Now present also in the Eucharistic liturgy of the Roman rite, it has become common in the recitation of the Lord's Prayer in ecumenical circles.

The explanation of the Lord's Prayer is divided into three brief articles. The first (nn. 2961-2976) presents the prayer as the center of the Scriptures, underlines its character as the fulfillment of revelation on prayer, and illustrates its Christological and pneumatological aspect. Its Trinitarian profile is stressed: it is the prayer of the Lord Jesus, addressed to the Father, inspired and always recreated by the Holy Spirit. Furthermore, in short treatises, it illustrates its ecclesial, communitarian, liturgical, eucharistic and eschatological character, according to the Church's Tradition and mind.

The second article (nn. 2777-2802) shows us the profound meaning of the initial words: "Our Father, who art in heaven". This invocation is often preceded in traditional ecclesial liturgy by an invitation to have courage and trust, to simplicity and filial sincerity, the evangelical *parrhesia* of the children who "dare" to call God Father. The word *Father* is explained in all its biblical depth in the light of many scriptural texts and Tradition, as the key to all prayer, in its twofold role of the revelation of God as Father and in the correct attitude of the one who prays in filial communion, filled with humility and trust.

The explanation of the adjective "our" opens the ecclesial and communal horizons of the Lord's Prayer and broadens its significance to a universality embracing humanity and all creation. In fact: "This divine anxiety for all people and for the whole of creation has inspired all the great people of prayer: it should extend our prayer to the immense spaces of love, when we venture to say 'our' Father', (n. 2793). The words "who art in heaven", remind us both of God's heavenly abode, his presence with us and our presence with him, as well as the status of the Christian who is the living temple of the Spirit, the place where God is present, according to an exegesis dear to the spiritual tradition of interior prayer.

The third article, the longest (nn. 2803-2865), briefly comments on each of the seven petitions of the Lord's Prayer. In this division the *Catechism of the Catholic Church* closely follows that of the *Roman Catechism*, putting before the explanation of the seven petitions the exegesis of the initial invocation: "Our Father, who art in heaven."

Everyone knows that the Lord's Prayer, including its initial invocation, is clearly divided into two sections, characterized by the prevalence of the "thou" addressed to God in praise and in invocation, and by the "we" which characterizes a series of requests. In reality, however, it always remains a dialogue between the "thou", (God) and the "we" (mankind) like a pendulum connecting heaven and earth.

A guide to understanding the seven petitions, preceded by invoking God as Father, is given by the *Catechism* in these words: "Having brought us into the presence of God our Father to adore him, to love him and to praise him, the filial Spirit makes seven requests; seven blessings rise from our hearts. The first three, which are more theological, draw us towards the glory of the Father; the last four, like four roads leading to him offer our poverty to his grace: 'Deep calls unto deep' (Ps 42: 8)" (n. 2803). The *Catechism* takes care to stress the doxological and theological character prevailing in the first three requests, and the aspect of supplication found in the last four, which concern the needs of our present life and the final and future victory.

Mary is the model of our prayer

For each of the seven requests, which the Mozarabic liturgy of Spain emphasizes and seals with a solemn "Amen", the

Catechism offers a biblical, ecclesial and spiritual explanation, furnished with appropriate commentaries from the liturgical and patristic tradition.

The meaning of hallowing God's Name, of the coming of the Kingdom and of doing God's Will is presented in beautiful summaries of great exegetical and spiritual value. In the requests for daily bread and the forgiveness of sins, apart from their exegetical and spiritual aspects, it stresses the commitments flowing from prayer, from trust in Providence to the necessity of work, from the request for mercy to total forgiveness and love of one's enemies as the highest form of charity.

The commentary explains the meaning of the request: "Lead us not into temptation." Taken literally, this expression means "do not let us give in to temptation": a petition which opens our hearts to the gifts of discernment and strength which are the work of the Holy Spirit and require strong decisions and constant vigilance. The last of the requests, with great realism, opens the discussion on evil and the Evil One, asking that we and everyone be fully liberated from them now and always.

The explanation of the Lord's Prayer concludes with a short note on the final doxology: "For the kingdom . . .." The *Catechism* appropriately comments that in this way we acknowledge that the kingdom, the power and the glory belong to God alone, while awaiting Christ to restore the kingdom to the Father, that he may be all in all.

The final "Amen" of the Lord's Prayer, to which the *Roman Catechism* had devoted a long annotation, is briefly explained by the *Catechism of the Catholic Church* in the words of Cyril of Jerusalem: "At the end of the prayer, you say, 'Amen', emphasizing with this: Amen, which means 'So be it', all that is contained in the prayer taught by God."

The careful reader of this last comment will not fail to observe a note referring to Lk 1: 38, that is, to Mary's reply to the angel at the annunciation: "Behold, I am the handmaid of the Lord. May it be done to me according to your word." Thus an implicit allusion is made to Mary as the model of the Church's prayer in her *Amen,* which is the "yes" of the new covenant.

In the Amen that ends the proclamation of the Lord's Prayer and concludes the *Catechism* we find the necessary, heartfelt assent of the whole Church to the faith that is proclaimed and professed, to the mystery of salvation that is celebrated, and to the spiritual life in Christ. In truth, the aim of all catechesis and of every catechism is to encourage an informed, loving, sincere adherence to the truth and to the life God gave us in his Son.

Cardinal Joseph Ratzinger stated: "Prayer without faith becomes blind; faith without prayer disintegrates." The Lord's Prayer has the merit of being both prayed faith and prayer steeped in faith, hope and love. Thus the Lord's Prayer is a profession of faith, a synthesis of prayer as supplication, praise and intercession, and also represents the baptismal commitment to new life.

XV

Catechism presents Scripture as revelation of God's salvific plan

Fr. Giuseppe Segalla
Pontifical Theological Commission

In order to understand the *remarkable novelty* of the conception and use of Scripture in the *Catechism of the Catholic Church*, one need only compare it with what is found in the preface of the *Catechismus Romanus* (1566): *"Omnis autem doctrinæ ratio quæ fidelibus tradenda sit verbo Dei continetur, quod in Scripturam Traditionesque distributum est"* (*Catechismus Romanus*, critical edition, Libreria Editrice Vaticana and University of Navarre, 1989, p. 12, n. 12).

The statement is followed by citing 1 Tm 4: 13 and 2 Tm 3: 16-17, exhorting pastors to a greater familiarity with Scripture, the source, together with "the Traditions", of Christian doctrine, inasmuch as they contain the word of God. And this is all there is on the subject.

The present *Catechism* embraces the enormous evolution that has taken place, especially during the last century in the way in which Scripture is viewed and used both by Christian people themselves (the biblical movement) and, correspondingly, by the Magisterium of the Church, from Leo XIII's *Providentissimus Deus* (1893) to the conciliar Constitution *Dei Verbum* on Divine Revelation (1965), although the latter document is the only one presented in the *Catechism*.

The following essay on the concept and use of Scripture in the *Catechism* will be limited to three points:

- Divine revelation, fulfilled in Christ, and Sacred Scripture;

- the importance of Scripture in the liturgy;
- the rich and varied use of Scripture in the exposition of Christian doctrine.

Divine revelation, fulfilled in Christ, and Scripture

The catechesis on Scripture is developed in the second chapter of the First Section (Part I: The Profession of Faith), entitled "I Believe-We Believe". Before speaking of the content of the faith (*fides quæ*), the believer is discussed in three stages:

- man in search of God;
- God reaches out to man, or divine revelation;
- and finally, man's response to God in faith.

In the second chapter (God reaches out to man) the Constitution on Divine Revelation *Dei Verbum* is taken up in catechetical form. Its six chapters are condensed into three articles:

- the revelation of God,
- its transmission
- and Scripture.

The first two correspond to the document's first two chapters, which bear the same title, while in the Third Part the remaining four chapters (Inspiration and interpretation, the Old Testament, the New Testament and Scripture in the life of the Church) are summarized more freely.

Divine revelation is viewed not only from the cognitive point of view as being another order of knowledge, superior to that of reason, but also from the personal viewpoint: "God reveals himself and *gives himself* to man by unveiling his mystery . . . " (n. 50).

Rather than insisting on the mystery of God in itself (the Trinitarian mystery actually pervades every profession of faith) *divine revelation* (Art. 1) is presented as a "benevolent plan" which is revealed in successive stages in history (from the beginning, the covenant with Noah, the election of Abraham and the formation of his people) all the way to its fulfillment in Christ Jesus, "the mediator and fullness of all revelation", for which reason there will never be another revelation.

The *transmission of divine revelation* (Art. 2) is more complex: the apostolic tradition, oral and written, continues through the living apostolic transmission (*Dei Verbum*, n. 8): the relationship between Tradition and Scripture is seen as that between the single divine source and two different modes of transmission: Tradition and Sacred Scripture (*Dei Verbum*, n. 9). With respect to *Dei Verbum*, however, the *Catechism* rightly observes (by the use of lower case) the difference between the apostolic Tradition, which is parallel to Scripture, and the ecclesial traditions which "consist in particular forms through which the great Tradition is expressed"; on the other hand the apostolic Tradition remains the criterion for distinguishing among the "traditions" as to which should be preserved, modified or even abandoned "under the guidance of the Magisterium".

This is a heuristic principle of great importance. Involved in interpreting the deposit of faith entrusted to the Church as a whole are, in the first place, the Magisterium of the Church, then the supernatural *sensus fidei* of the believers in union with their Bishops, and finally, growth in the understanding of the faith (*Dei Verbum* n. 10).

Against this background of divine revelation, transmitted and interpreted, *Sacred Scripture* (Art. 3) is presented as a privileged mode in the transmission of revelation. The exposition is articulated in five points:

1) Christ—the unique Word (*Dei Verbum*, nn. 10, 3), spoken by God "through all the words of Scripture";

2) the inspiration and truth of Scripture;

3) the Holy Spirit, interpreter of Scripture;

4) the canon of the Scriptures, in which are synthesized Chapters 4 and 5 of *Dei Verbum*;

5) Sacred Scripture in the life of the Church (Chapter 6 of *Dei Verbum*).

I limit myself to pointing out the novelty with respect to *Dei Verbum*, concentrated above all in points 3 and 4.

Rather than speaking of "the way to interpret Scripture" (*Dei Verbum*, n. 12), which favors the anthropological aspect, the *Catechism* brings out the theological aspect, with the title of "the Holy Spirit, interpreter of Scripture". Just as Scripture was inspired by the Spirit, so it must be interpreted by the same Spirit. In connection with the human-divine nature of Scripture ("God speaks to man in a human manner . . . [through] the sacred writers": n. 109) interpretation should include an effort to understand *the intention of the sacred writers* by means of all the necessary historical-exegetical tools (n. 110); but, and even more importantly, it must also try to grasp the intention of the Holy Spirit who is its principal author.

It is on this second, divine side of the issue that the *Catechism* dwells at length. And, for teaching purposes, it formulates *three criteria* for interpreting Scripture "in conformity with the Holy Spirit":

- to pay attention "to the contents and unity of the whole of Scripture" (theological-canonical criterion);

- to read Scripture in the "living tradition of the whole Church" (ecclesial criterion, where, in my opinion, "tradition" should be understood in the sense of "ecclesial traditions", as distinct from apostolic Tradition, which is referred to in n. 83);

- to be attentive to the "analogy of faith", that is, to the coherence of the truths of faith with one another (the properly theological criterion).

There is a brief reference to the senses of Scripture "according to an ancient tradition": the famous four senses, within a twofold structure (the literal sense and the threefold spiritual sense). In conclusion, n. 119 enunciates the necessary task of exegetes within the Church and her horizon.

The *Canon of the Scriptures* (nn. 120-127) first of all lists the books of the Old and New Testaments. The permanent value of the Old Testament as the word of God is affirmed against both ancient and modern forms of Marcionism. Concerning the New Testament it stresses that the Gospels are "the heart of Scripture" and there is a brief reminder regarding the three stages of formation (the historical Jesus, tradition and redaction) according to *Dei Verbum*, n. 19, which refers the reader to the short Instruction *Sacrosancta Mater Ecclesia* (*AAS* 56 [1964]: 715).

The theological consequence of the sacred canon is the unity of the Old and New Testaments, which should be fostered through a typological reading of the Old Testament in the light of Christ who is the fulfillment of the divine plan. Such an interpretation of the Old Testament is already begun in the New and is continued in scriptural interpretation down the centuries, although in diverse forms. This passage appears to sanction the idea that one can write a "biblical theology", that is, a theology of the whole Bible, but only by taking the New Testament as the starting point for reading the Old (cf. G. Segalla, *Panorama teologico del Nuovo Testamento*, Brescia 1987, pp. 31-33).

In conclusion, the conception of Scripture expressed in the *Catechism* is substantially that of *Dei Verbum* with a strong emphasis, however, on the "God reaches out to man" aspect (the chapter title), that is, on God's role and that of the Spirit both in the origin of Scripture and in its "spiritual" interpretation in the Church, and on the role of the Word incarnate as the fulfillment of revelation.

Scripture as the living word of God in liturgy and in prayer

Glancing at the thematic index, one observes that, besides the long treatment which we have just analyzed, the expression "Holy Scripture" later recurs in the section on the celebration of the Christian mystery (Part II) and in that on Christian prayer (Part IV):

- Above all in the treatment of the sacraments (n. 1117), which have been determined by ecclesial tradition in a way analogous to the definition of the canon;

- Moreover, the primary symbol of the Eucharistic liturgy is seen in the episode of the disciples on the road to Emmaus (n. 1347). First Jesus himself explains to them the mystery of his death-resurrection by interpreting the Scriptures, then he celebrates a meal with them. So it is in the Eucharistic liturgy too. Christ is thus "present in his word, since it is he who speaks when the Holy Scriptures are read in the Church" (n. 1088).

- Finally, the reading of Scripture should be accompanied by prayer (n. 2653), which forms the heart of the Liturgy of the Hours, in particular the psalms (n. 2762).

In conclusion, the privileged place in which Scripture becomes a living and effective word is the liturgy, in particular that of the Eucharist.

The rich and varied use of Scripture

In its use and interpretation of Scripture is the *Catechism* faithful to the theoretical principles expounded above? The response to this question is a resounding "yes".

I would like first of all to call the reader's attention to the *abundance* of biblical citations, which outnumber all the others. If we take a look at the index of citations: in the French edition 30 of the 58 pages are devoted to citations from Scripture and in the Italian edition, 26 of 48, more than half. All the books of the New Testament are cited; special attention is given to the Gospels, "the heart of Scripture" and, among these, Matthew (the ecclesial-catechetical Gospel) and John (the most theological) are especially favored.

All the books of the Old Testament are also cited with the exception of four of the minor prophets (Habakkuk, Obadiah, Haggai and Nahum); the only surprise here is the absence of Habakkuk because Hb 2: 4 is an important text in the New Testament for expressing the faith that saves (Gal 3: 11; Rom 1: 17; Heb 10: 37-38).

The original text is almost always favored, but with a few exceptions, where the text of the Septuagint is cited (nn. 59 and 462) or that of the Vulgate (in n. 1832, Gal 5: 22-23, because the Vulgate text here lists 12 fruits of the Holy Spirit instead of nine, and this list has become part of traditional catechesis). The biblical text therefore is cited by taking into account the living tradition, of which the first form is the translation used in the liturgy: the Septuagint in the Judeo-Hellenistic world and the Vulgate in the Roman Church.

The references to Scripture are consistently accurate because the text was carefully reviewed by experts in the Old and New Testaments prior to its final draft.

What use is made of Scripture? By and large, I would say that a *canonical usage* is practiced, in the sense that Scripture is viewed as a unified book, the book of God. Thus Old Testament texts are cited together which are quite far apart from the historical-literary point of view, or texts of the Old and New Testaments that have to do with the same subject are brought together.

A unity is thus imposed by the one plan of God and by the one Author of Scripture. Let me cite one example: "Creation, the work of the Blessed Trinity" (nn. 290-292). In n. 290 "creation" is spoken of as an act proper to God, this thesis likewise has a biblical foundation in the observation that the Hebrew verb *bara* (to create) in Scripture always has God for its subject. N. 291 speaks of the Word-Son as the Mediator of creation and this is illustrated by putting together Jn 1: 1-3 and Col 1: 16-17; for the Spirit as Creator appeal is made instead to the Tradition of the Church. The creative action of the Son and the Spirit is merely "hinted at" in the Old Testament (Ps 33: 6; 104: 30; Gn 1: 2-3), but this inference can be made only through a "Christian" reading.

Within this generalized canonical use of Scripture one could specify *four different ways of referring to Scripture*, which we will briefly outline.

- The first and most evident is *the explicit citation*, as in the example just mentioned. Wherever possible, the *Catechism* begins a chapter or an article with a scriptural citation (cf. n. 1077 at the beginning of the sacramental economy; nn. 1092-95 in the introduction to "Life in Christ"; n. 1701, which begins the article "Man as image of God", etc.). In the exposition of Christian doctrine Old and New Testament texts are referred to, usually but not always in their distinct contexts, but in any case without any historical-literary concern, which should presumably be the object of a specific catechesis: biblical catechesis.

- More extensive is the use of *reference citations* (indicated by an asterisk in the biblical index), which are given in the footnotes in order to simplify the text. A note in the preface explains their function: "Often, a text of Sacred Scripture is not cited literally: only the reference is supplied (with cf.). For an in-depth understanding of such passages one is advised to go to the text itself. These biblical references constitute a useful tool for catechesis" (n. 19).

- A third way of reading Scripture comes closer to the *exegesis of a text*, even employing the historical-critical method in a measured way. This manner of approaching biblical texts is found, for example, in the Decalogue and above all in the explanation of the "Lord's Prayer". Here, besides philology, reference is likewise made to literary criticism which distinguishes between the Lucan redaction and that of Matthew (n. 2759), but without appealing to literary theories which are still the subject of debate, such as the "Q source". It is interesting to note, however, that even in this case, exegesis in the strict sense is enriched by an attempt to capture the text's resonances in ecclesial tradition: patristic and liturgical. The final draft of the commentary on the "Lord's Prayer" was fortunately simplified in comparison with the first draft which contained an overly extended exegesis. This catechetical use of exegesis, modest as it is, shows the contribution biblical science can make when it limits itself to noting reliable literary data and making intelligent use of them.

- The most frequent and less evident use of Scripture is perhaps comparable to the *soul*, which permeates the whole and gives life to the whole, without itself being seen. It is the use of words, expressions, biblical figures, even without explicit citation or reference, as is done already in the New Testament, e.g., in the Book of Revelation. Scripture in this case is not only the "great reference text" to assist understanding, but also the inner dynamism which makes the discourse of faith relevant and alive. For a brilliant example of this fourth mode of using Scripture one might read "Prayer in the Christian life", the First Section of Part IV.

Concluding reflections

Following the model of the "In brief" found at the end of each article, I would also like to summarize what I have said by highlighting three facts of great importance in the Catechism's conception and use of Scripture.

- The *Catechism* expounds, in a didactic way, the teaching of *Dei Verbum* on Sacred Scripture: the Old and New Testaments as the revelation of God's plan for man and as "God's book", written under the inspiration of the Spirit, and interpreted with the assistance of the same Spirit, taking into account, however, the human mediation of the sacred writers and thus not hesitating to employ the historical-critical method.

  At the same time that it confesses Scripture as the "book of God", however, it forcefully denies that Christianity is a "religion of the Book" (n. 108). And it continues: "Christianity is the religion of the 'Word of God' not a written and mute word, but the incarnate and living Word." In our cultural context, such an assertion assumes the greatest importance as a definition setting off the Christian faith from every form of biblical fundamentalism and from every arteriosclerosis of the word of God.

- The word of Scripture then is the "living word" of the living God, which must always be listened to anew, interpreted and applied in the changing situations of time and different cultures. For this reason the *Catechism*, while looking to the original text, will frequently refer as well to the official translations used in the liturgy, such as the Septuagint and the Vulgate. It hardly needs to be said that the most primary form of interpretation is translation itself.

- The result of the catechetical effort displayed in the use of Scripture is to reduce the tension between the historical sense of the text (what the text *meant*), which is, however, usually respected, and the present meaning (what the text *means* today), since Scripture is read within the context of the living tradition (patristic, liturgical, hagiographical, magisterial) and in the light of today's culture. The weight falls obviously on the present meaning, but always in conjunction with the original sense.

For example, the section entitled "Man and woman he created them" (nn. 369-373) reflects the feminist problem in a balanced, concise and intelligent way, with the altered man-woman relationship that is its consequence, in relation to God as Creator, "mother and father". To be noted also is the final reference to man's responsibility to God for the created world in n. 373, an idea which is complemented by nn. 307 and 2415.

Not all contemporary problems can be read in Scripture, however, although they can all be illuminated by principles drawn from it. For example, in Chapter 2 of Part III: "The human community", the source to which the *Catechism* appeals is chiefly the recent Magisterium and there one finds only a rare citation of the Bible. Here it is possible to measure the historical-cultural limits of Scripture which must be respected. At the time the Bible was written neither modern democracy nor socialization were in existence.

By way of summary, one could say that Scripture in the *Catechism* is read and interpreted as the living Word of the living God (Father, Son and Holy Spirit) for man, the Church and the world of today.

XVI

Catechism points to Mary as the mother and example of the faithful

Lila B. Archideo
Servidora

The striking early third-century image of our Lady placed at the beginning of the *Catechism* prepares our hearts and minds, through the example of the strength of the Mother of the Church, to receive the *Catechism*: to enlighten, guide and nourish each Christian's desire for holiness and to offer all people a lively synthesis of the effectiveness of faith, hope and charity upon which the Catholic Church is founded.

The faith of the Christian and the work of the pastor, the theologian and the catechist meet in a profound Mariology which, inspired by the texts of the Old Testament, unites with those of the New, of which the Virgin Mary is the open door; this Mariology recurs as the source of inspiration from the Council of Ephesus to Vatican II and in the Encyclicals of the many Popes who expounded the Marian theme, up to *Redemptoris Mater* and *Mulieris Dignitatem*. The apostolic tradition and patrology are summarized, as are the writings of the saints who were inspired by and, in turn, acknowledge the one who gave her total response to God. The Eastern liturgy allows us to taste the delicacy of the Byzantine *troparia*. The Roman Ritual and the Western Liturgy of the Hours provide a similar experience, as do other texts of this synthetic and foundational Mariology.

The presence of Mary—the Mother who silently guides and watches over the path of her pilgrim child, providing whatever he needs, and giving herself—is constant in the *Catechism.* After every important statement one is tempted to add: *like the Blessed Virgin.*

The editors have clearly indicated at every step Mary's exemplariness, and they state it explicitly in what is essential.

She appears to light man's path on earth, showing the Christian sacramental way of life united to her *sacramentality:* that of the one who is privileged to belong entirely to Christ alone.

The Mother of God and the Christian's faith

The *Catechism* outlines how God forms his priestly people through the prophets and the holy women (cf. n. 64). Before dealing with the Mediator and the fullness of all Revelation, it makes us contemplate and appreciate the purest figure, Mary, the instrument essential to the definitive covenant, the ultimate Revelation. In the section on obedience to the faith, with which the Creed begins the text explains: "The Virgin Mary is its most perfect realization" (n. 144), because "in faith she received the message and the promise brought to her by the angel Gabriel, believing that 'nothing is impossible for God' (Lk 1: 37)." Her virginity appears as the distinctive sign of her faith, her total response to God. "Because of this faith all ages will call her blessed", because her faith did not waver. "So much so that in Mary the Church venerates the most perfect realization of the faith"; in her pilgrimage *she emerges from "the dark night" of faith* as an example of the battle that we Christians must wage, and from which we must emerge strengthened, "always keeping our attention fixed on Jesus", who begins and brings to completion the Christian faith (cf. n. 165).

As we go through the articles of the Creed in the *Catechism*, we cannot fail to recognize the greatest witness to seeking the divine: she of the "righteous heart" who from her youth sought God and through him Beauty, Love and Truth, and who cherished in her heart the Old Testament, to arrive *at the only book: Jesus Christ.* "Blessed is she who believed" (cf. n. 148) with complete freedom, because by her humility she was called to fill the emptiness of self with God.

Faith in the incarnation

Like a symphony of creation the figure of Mary, the Mother of God-made-man, permits us to hear with human ears and hearts the sweet harmony of an earthly voice joined to heaven: thus the incarnation of God begins. Anthropology is enriched with divine features, giving fullness to man and to history.

Thus Mary is transformed into the living sanctuary bearing the divine Person of the Lord from his conception until birth, forming within her finite womb the sacrament of the Infinite. What God wants to show us is that he seeks the fullness of obedience, so that his desire for the salvation of humanity, for which he prepared with the old covenant, is fulfilled through the fullness of grace: he seeks virginity for the fullness of motherhood.

The Word was made flesh . . . : the Niceno-Constantinopolitan Creed, St. John (1: 14) and St. Paul (Phil 2: 5 8) are quoted so that we may contemplate the masterpiece of creation in the *chiaroscuro* of the mystery of the Virgin-Mother, and they speak words inspired by the Spirit. We are face to face with the Mother of Jesus, true God and true man.

And the Mariological theme continues, showing the wealth which the Church proclaims in her faith and lives in her liturgy, the divine lesson revealed to us in the incarnation and afterwards, in the pregnancy and nativity, the sanctifying mission of the Holy Spirit and his fruitful mission in the womb of the Virgin Mary—which had already been active at her immaculate conception. Similarly, the Spirit sanctifies and makes fruitful the Church, which finds her model in Mary: the Trinity prepared Mary from eternity, just as it prepares each Christian for his or her mission.

The teaching about Mary enlightens the faith in Jesus—the *Catechism* explains to us—because our faith in the Mother is based on what the Church believes about the Lord.

She who is full of grace from her conception is redeemed by God before the cross, by the merits of her Son, because Jesus' redemption, wrapped in the mystery of the Love of God, expresses the totally free *fiat* of Mary, who responds with the "obedience of faith" to the call and mission that the Almighty entrusts to her, putting herself at the service of redemption.

The *Catechism* calls on St. Ignatius of Antioch, St. Irenæus and many Fathers of the Latin and Greek Churches to testify to the maternity of the ever Virgin; in the same way the Councils and Popes are also called upon.

The mystery of the Virgin-Mother is the plan of God which the *Catechism*, by means of the Church's pedagogy based on the divine, enables us to live by the assent of faith and the peace of the prayer of centuries; it enlightens our reason, inspires our hearts and expands our Christian freedom.

Mary and Redemption

The Virgin, for her part, is the most sublime fruit of the Redemption in which she cooperated *in faith and obedience.*

She said her *fiat* in the name of humanity, as the *Catechism* tells us, successfully condensing a much longer explanation. With necessary precision and methodology, the editors offer us at each step of this sacramental text of the Church summaries that are full of methodological and dogmatic wealth.

The catechetical text continues with the mysteries of the life of Christ, where the Virgin is the silent Christian contemplating and cooperating with her prayer and, in this, with her whole life.

During the Lord's passion, crucifixion, death, and burial, as well as his "descent into hell", she is virtually or explicitly present as the one who cooperates in redemption: at his resurrection and ascension into heaven, as the faithful witness of a love that has no equal; in the descent of the Spirit, by which we are permitted to know all that concerns God, Mary is *full of grace.*

The *Catechism* presents the work of the mission of the Word, of the Holy Spirit and the desires of the Father. It assigns to the Trinitarian family the first outline of this marvel that is Christ, of which he himself will complete the design.

Through Mary, the Spirit manifests the Son of the eternal Father and begins to place mankind in communion with God.

The Apostles and the Spirit inaugurate the Church on Pentecost and she is there because she precedes us all *on the path
of holiness:* "the Marian dimension of the Church precedes the
Petrine dimension" (n. 773).

Mary, Mother of Christ and of the Church

In the section on the Church, Mary is the first in holiness, and
the Church's activity is thus modelled on her again: the
Church, People of God, Body of Christ, Temple of the Spirit.
St. Clement of Alexandria shows the already total holiness of
the Church in Mary, the point of departure and of arrival for
the *raison d'être* of her structure: Pope, Bishops, priests,
consecrated persons and laity in communion with heaven
and earth.

Having followed her in her silent prayer, the *Catechism* bursts
out in praise of her motherhood of the Church in the mystery
of Christ (cf. nn. 963-975) and, in union with Jesus, covers the
mystery of her life, joining her role as Mother of the Mystical
Body to her role as mother of the Lord.

Mary's role as model, the heart of the Catechism's teaching, is
made explicit, and her mediation and blessedness exalt that of
her Son.

Her attitude as the handmaid of the Lord and the perfect
accomplishment of her mission make her "an eminent and
absolutely unique member of the Church", and in her
exemplary fulfillment, she rightly becomes the *archetype.* She
was so from her birth until her death and, since her assump-
tion, until the end of time she will be the mother, advocate
and mediatrix (cf. *Lumen Gentium,* nn. 62, 65).

For this reason the Church's devotion to her mother "is
intrinsic to Christian devotion" and the pilgrim people of God
see in her the sign of hope (cf. *Marialis Cultus,* nn. 56, 42).

Eschatology finds in Mary the one who led a perfect life on earth
and entered into eternal life, where she shares in the glory of her
Son and anticipates our resurrection, while she continues to
guide us as our Mother until we meet *our sister death* (St. Francis

of Assisi, "Canticle of the Creatures"). Thus she helps us in the supreme moment (*Roman Ritual*, "Commendation of the Dying") with her faith in the resurrection of the body and in eternal life, and she gives us the courage to ask pardon for our sins and to raise our eyes to heaven so that we can enter into a perfect communion of life and love with the Blessed Trinity, with her, the angels, and all the saints (cf. n. 1024).

Mary and the celebration of the Christian mystery

The liturgy, the work of the Trinity, shows us the praise of sons and daughters. The Mother is there with the earthly liturgy, which is a participation in the heavenly one. The Book of Revelation is quoted by the *Catechism* with regard to the eternal praise of all creation with Mary (cf. n. 1138). The earth is full of images of the Mother, which speak of the Son, acknowledge his primary glory and recall her throughout the liturgical year (cf. nn. 1161-1162).

And when the offering of the cross is renewed on the altar of the Eucharistic sacrifice, "the Church, with Mary, is as it were at the foot of the Cross, united to the offering and the intercession of Christ" (n. 1370).

The sacraments, which in faith confer grace, recall the one who was "obedient in faith" and "full of grace", and thus continue the image of her veiled but active role as example.

The sacraments of Baptism and Confirmation recall the Jewish maiden's total consecration and the sacrament of Penance recalls her cooperation in redemption. The sacrament of the Eucharist refers to the living sanctuary, which she never left, while waiting in faith for the Son of her womb; it recalls her motherhood of this Body and Blood while responding to Christ's coming on the altar, as once he came into her womb, through the Holy Spirit.

The Anointing of the Sick places her at the bedside of the person who is approaching eternal life and blesses that passing; Orders finds her in the intimate maternity of those who participate in the priesthood of her Son; Matrimony— which recalls Mary's sensitivity at the wedding feast of Cana (cf. n. 1613)—alludes to the exemplary love of the Mother, Spouse of the Word and Mother of the Church, Bride of Christ, to which tile sacrament refers as a sign (cf. n. 1617).

The sacramentals silently emphasize the power of the Mother who accompanies her Church and helps in daily life; popular piety acknowledges her presence in all peoples, with the wisdom of the humble and the power of creative genius.

Mary and life in Christ

A life of dignity, under the inspiration of the Spirit, is the life of the Christian according to the Beatitudes. In her humility, Mary knew from the beginning, through her union with Jesus, that she would be *blessed*, an example for all people. A blessedness that the Virgin inaugurates with her life, showing us the path of the Church, on which each Christian is fulfilled in his or her vocation.

Mary is the sign which gives guidance and direction toward the ultimate goal throughout all the temporal activity of man, whether individual or social.

In her the law appears as divine Providence, summarizing the life of the Mosaic law and the new law of love.

In the *Magnificat* the commandments relating to God are exemplified and praise is centered in him, so that the prayer rises to her Son (cf. n. 2097).

In a special passage the *Catechism* describes the veneration of the Church's children: "The veneration of sacred images is based on the mystery of the incarnation of the Word of God" (n. 2141) and reminds the Christian of his relationship with God and neighbor, moral and material life. In this veneration, sacred art exalts "the spiritual beauty reflected in the Blessed Virgin Mary, Mother of God."

Christian prayer: prayer in communion with Mary

Through Mary's total obedience in the faith, the *Catechism* shows us that prayer is the lever with which the finite moves the Infinite. With Mary the Latin *Magnificat* or the Byzantine *Megalynarion* represents the prayer of the Church the profound hymn of the spirit, in which she commits herself totally to the Lord even before his incarnation, in the prayer of the one who "cooperated in a unique manner in the benign plan of the Father." The prayer of the Virgin Mary (cf. nn. 2617, 2619) moves heaven and earth.

When Jesus allows us to glimpse the unfathomable depth of prayer at the Last Supper, preceding the moment of the ultimate fulfillment of the Father's will, he remembers Mary; it is to her that he turns on the cross, and makes of the Virgin the praying Mother, thus giving us the gift which sustains us in continual prayer (cf. n. 2605).

And when at the same supper he gives us his Body and Blood to eat, with the Church, he constitutes Mary in the power of the Eucharistic Prayer: "It is a communion of intercession with the Most Holy Mother of God" (n. 2827).

The *Catechism* notes that the way of prayer enters into communion with the Mother of God because Jesus designated her as our Mother (cf. nn. 2673, 2682).

The exemplary faith of our Mother, by the power of her *fiat*, proclaims the essential prayer which embraces all paths, the 'yes' to the call and the mission, and "the individual cooperation with the action of the Holy Spirit", which every Christian must contemplate in her.

The Church, ever faithful to the Lord, manifests in her hymns and antiphons her praise and confidence in her petitions to the Mother. Together with the *Magnificat*, the Church offers the *Ave Maria*. It is a heavenly voice spoken by a human one and, at the same time, it is the heavenly greeting of the angel: full of grace, blessed is the fruit of your womb, and the earthly greeting of Elizabeth to the Mother of God (cf. n. 2676).

The Liturgy of the Hours and then the popular Rosary in the West, the litany form of the *Akathist* and the *Paraclesis* in the East (n. 2678), the Byzantine office, the hymns and the canticles of the Armenians, the Copts and the Syrians are united by the same essential tradition: "Mary is the perfect *Orans*, the figure of the Church" (n. 2679).

In every place of prayer to the Lord the image of the Virgin reminds us that she is the guide and guarantee of our prayer because she led a life of prayer, she meditated unceasingly, she conquered evil with her prayer, she placed her trust and her continuous vigilance in Jesus.

The "Our Father" synthesizes the virtual or explicit prayer of Mary before and after her Son taught his disciples, and therefore all of us, how to pray.

Prayer requires faith, hope and love; it makes supplication for spiritual and material necessities, it assures liberation from the devil who, powerless against the Mother who is "full of grace", becomes angry "with the woman" and goes off "to wage war against the rest of her offspring" (Rv 12: 17) (cf. n. 2853). But she is capable of more than all the powers of evil: she is the supplicating omnipotence that obtains the victory that fills with strength and transforms into freedom the Christian's earthly struggle to gain eternal happiness.

The *Catechism* constantly has us bow our heads in love and gratitude so as to rest them on her motherly breast and arouses the deepest sentiments of our heart towards our Mother by antonomasia, the principal analogical reality of all Christian life.

When he presented the *Catechism*, the Holy Father asked "the Blessed Virgin Mary, Mother of the Incarnate Word and Mother of the Church, to support with her powerful intercession the catechetical work of the entire Church on every level, at this time when she is called to a new effort of evangelization" (John Paul II, *Fidei Depositum*, n. 5).

In the way it is written the *Catechism of the Catholic Church* shows us by the Marian dogmas the Blessed Virgin's exemplary role in every dimension of the life of humanity, whose mother she is, and emphasizes for us the divine features and the fruitfulness of the human response in that masterpiece which God gives to man to show us his Beauty, so that attracted by her we may reach him. Thus, the *Catechism* is also a Marian gift to the Church.

XVII

Formulas should be adapted to needs and capacity of audience

Mgr. Raffaello Martinelli
Official of the Congregation for the Doctrine of the Faith

The *Catechism of the Catholic Church* presents some brief formulas which summarize, in simple and concise form, important topics concerning the belief, celebrations, way of life and prayer of the Catholic Church. In the French text they are called "*En bref*".

According to necessity or when merely opportune, they are placed at the end of the sections, chapters or articles that are of particular importance in Christian doctrine.

Characteristics

Among the characteristics of these formulas, the following should be noted:

- As brief formulas, those which are the *cornerstones of the four-part structure* of the *Catechism* should be considered first of all: part one, the creeds (the Apostles' Creed explained in the light of the Niceno-Constantinopolitan Creed); part two, the sacraments; part three, the commandments (as well as the beatitudes and the virtues); part four, the Lord's Prayer.

  These cornerstones, which continue one of the most widespread and ancient catechetical traditions (cf. the *Roman Catechism*), allow Catholic doctrine to be explained, arranging it in an organic, systematic and hierarchical manner, emphasizing its essential and basic complementary contents.

- The contents of the "*En bref*", formulas preferably come from *biblical, liturgical, patristic and magisterial sources and from testimonies.* This emphasizes the close connection and circular complementarity between the above-mentioned Christian sources, which enlighten and explain one another, while leading to an ever deeper and clearer understanding and explanation of the Christian mystery. Thus a wise choice can be seen, an enriching symbiosis of continuity and newness in terms of Catholic doctrine.

- They *summarize the essentials* of Catholic doctrine, which the Catholic Church proclaims, celebrates, lives and prays. They seek to encapsulate the doctrinal substance "*tam de fide quam de moribus*". For this reason great effort has been made to avoid, wherever possible, including in the formulas, elements relating to the subject matter but referring to theories, opinions or theological hypothesis which should rather be found in reviews, debates and theological schools but not incorporated in a catechism (cf. *Catechesi Tradendæ*, n. 61), and especially not in this *Catechism.*

- They are furthermore closely *related to the respective paragraphs* which precede each of them.

  With regard to the manner of obtaining and expressing the indissoluble link between them (text) and the paragraphs (context) which precede them and which illustrate Christian doctrine on a given theme, the editors had several options to choose from, which basically were narrowed down to two: either to enlarge on what had already been said, or to limit themselves to summarizing it.

  When asked explicitly about this, the committee which the Holy Father appointed to draft the *Catechism* indicated to the editors that they should avoid using the formulas to introduce new elements that are doctrinally important and which would not be already present in the preceding paragraphs. They invited them to restate in the formulas, in concise form, what had been previously stated explicitly or implicitly.

- Considering the extreme importance of language in imparting catechesis, particular attention was paid to the type of language used in the concise formulas and generally throughout the *Catechism.* The editors preferred what is called the language of witness, which permits the explanation of the Church's faith in a manner that is positive rather than negative, calm rather than polemical, based on witness rather than on argument. The result is a catechetical presentation which better responds to the demands of the new evangelization and to the expectations of people today.

• While they are presented as suitable for being committed to memory, the formulas, which the *Catechism* offers as explanatory models summarizing the Catholic faith, because of their very nature and the intentions often explicitly expressed by their editors, require *further and indispensable adaptation.* They need an appropriate and complementary mediation, depending on personal needs and the specific capacities of those for whom they are intended. This is necessary both for achieving the goals set for these formulas in the *Catechism of the Catholic Church* and to respect the particular characteristics of various cultures, of the multiform individual Churches, of the variety of types of people for whom they are intended.

This work of adaptation, mediation and inculturation is carried out at different levels:

— In the first place by the *editors of local, national and diocesan catechisms.* Every language has its own character-istics regarding the terms used, its rhythm, cadence and "music". Every culture, every language uses various means and expedients, literary and poetic devices, to facilitate the various phases of the process involved in the individual's ability to memorize: rote learning, retention, recall and reformulation. In the light of these require-ments and usages, it is absolutely necessary for the editors of local catechisms to adapt appropriately the doctrinal content expressed in the formulas proposed by the *Catechism of the Catholic Church.*

— However, the *catechist* must also intelligently adapt and use these formulas. When presenting the formulas to be memorized, he must take into account both their position and their importance in the objective, organic and systematic layout of the Christian mystery, and the concrete subjective capacity of the recipient, of his psychology, of his existential vocation and situation, of the rate and significant stages of his growth, of the sociocultural context to which he belongs and of the level of faith which he has attained . . . . It is a question of offering the person being catechized those formulas which "in a particular context can be integrated into the thoughts and lives of the listeners", proposing them according to the situation and duties of each one" (St. Thomas, *Summa theologiæ*, II-II, q. 2, a. 7).

— Gradualness, loyalty to the centrality of the individual, a clever and careful selection with respect for the completeness of the mystery and the subject's concrete relational situation; these are but a few of the guiding criteria which should enlighten and inspire the catechist's work. Respecting and pursuing all this is part of the wisdom and art of being and acting as a catechist.

Goals

The goals at which these formulas aim are many yet complementary:

- *As for the "depositum fidei"*: their aim is to express essentially and succinctly the doctrinal content of the Christian faith, helping to determine the fundamental concept that the Christian faith proposes regarding a particular theme.

Taken together, these formulas permit the encapsulation of that indispensable "minimum" (*"non omnia sed totum"*), which every Catholic, in order to be such, must know, live and give witness to.

They stress the simplicity (without being simplistic) and at the same time the complex versatility of the Christian mystery, which in its unfathomable richness and its wonderful articulation appears in a unitary and concise manner to the individual who receives it in faith.

They also permit the rewording of the substance of the Christian faith in a more up-to-date language that fully involves the modern person.

— By distinguishing within the area of Catholic doctrine what is fundamental, essential, and unchangeable from what is secondary, transitory and peripheral, they promote an organic arrangement of the contents and the truths of the faith.

They emphasize the fact that all the catechetical contents lead back to and reconnect with "a central nucleus where everything must be driven by a centrifugal force and returned by a centripetal force, and the center is called: Jesus" (Pius XII, Speech of 11 January 1953). Thus meaning and a hierarchy of values are bestowed on the different statements, integrating new elements with those already acquired, avoiding the dissipation of the true proclamation in a series of concepts, doctrines and information without any respect for the structure and organic unity of the Christian mystery, of its essential nature and incisiveness.

This arrangement, which makes allowance for the position which each truth occupies in the architecture of the Christian mystery and which expresses the link with the central source, foundation and inspiration, recalls the close circular connection which exists between: the mystery of God and the mystery of the person; the Word of God and human experience; basic transcendental problems and contingent situations; the Bible-Tradition-Magisterium of the Church and the human sciences.

— The search for doctrinal precision and a genuine, complete formulation of the Christian truth, which characterized the elaboration of these formulas, has contributed and continues to increase the knowledge of the Christian mystery, to render more explicit a truth which is already contained in germ in the revealed truth, to re-express in a way that is more accessible to the modern mentality the eternal meaning of the assertion of faith.

Therefore through these formulas both the perception of reality and of the transmitted divine word grows as does their communication and transmission.

- *With regard to the readers*: These formulas, which belong to a sound and appropriate pedagogy of the faith, guide the personal itinerary of faith, with a view to reaching full Christian ecclesial maturity.

The definitive aim in fact of catechesis, and therefore of the catechetical formulas, "is to put people not only in touch but in communion, in intimacy with Jesus Christ: only he can lead us to the love of the Father in the Spirit and make us share in the life of the holy Trinity" (*Catechesi Tradendæ*, n. 5). "The whole purpose of doctrine and teaching must be placed in never-ending love" (Council of Trent, Art. X).

The catechetical formulas therefore involve the whole person: they favor the growth, from the point of view of knowledge, of the seed of faith placed by the Holy Spirit with the first proclamation and catechesis; they offer concrete means for "professing the faith" at a personal and community level; they invite one to a sincere conversion of heart; they direct the transformation of the individual's life so that, in following Christ he may think, judge, love and act according to his word.

While they excite and sustain convictions and attitudes of faith, at the same time they represent the occasions, moments and contents of dialogue with God through personal and community prayer. These concise expressions, many of which manifest an uncommon literary beauty, nourish and foster prayer, becoming guides to and in prayer.

With regard then to the person who is approaching the faith for the first time and wishes to learn the essential and fundamental truths which belong to the Catholic Church, they offer the chance for a simple and essential approach.

— The brief summaries also offer starting points for further investigation of the Christian truth. Inasmuch as they are directed towards the intellectual faculty of the human person (*"fides quærens intellectum"*), through the rediscovery of the reasons of the faith, they encourage a rational investigation into the contents of the faith, a doctrinal penetration of it, which can be carried out through the forms of inquiry and reflection that belong to thought. This reflection can take place in different ways depending on the individual, but also in successive moments by the same person, with that gradualness that mirrors the growth of the person in the different phases of his life, in the various circumstances of his existence.

- *With regard to the catholicity of the Church*: The catechetical formulas appear as a concrete, though always insufficient, instrument of communion in the one faith.

In a multicultural, pluralist and secularized world, one sees the need, with ever greater and more widespread insistence, to be united with other believers in Christ to enucleate, profess and testify to the one faith in different environments, continents and situations. This desire finds a concrete and effective instrument for its accomplishment in the *Catechism*, and in particular in the brief formulas.

What the Holy Spirit has intimated to the Church throughout the centuries and in different places, through her pastors and in her faithful by means of intellectual reflection, prayerful meditation, devout celebration, active charity and courageous testimony, is collected and arranged in a concise and organic form, to be committed to the "memory" of present and future generations, thus realizing that synchronic and diachronic communion which characterizes the existence and the activity of the Church. An important aid is thus furnished, precisely through the acquisition and utilization of a common language of faith, which is transmitted by these formulas, to promote, express and guarantee that unity of the Church's faith (*communio sanctorum*) which is the fruit and reflection of the Trinitarian unity.

While the formulas express the doctrinal content correctly, although imperfectly and incompletely, in a language that takes into account today's cultural context, by proposing a common manner of professing the faith, they signify and promote the catholicity of the Church, which is, "all the world's languages united in one single liturgy, or a melodious chorus sustained by the voices of unnumbered multitudes, rising in countless modulations, tones and harmonies for the praise of God from every part of the globe, at every moment in history" (John Paul II, *Slavorum Apostoli* n. 17).

• *With regard to catechetical activity*: Among the many important benefits which the formulas bring to catechetical activity both from the point of view of teaching and from that of learning (to avoid being haphazard and fragmentary both in proclaiming and receiving the faith), the following should not be underestimated: the formulas permit the catechist to test the capacity and level of learning of the one receiving the proclamation (the person who is being catechized). Through this "feedback" technique, the catechist also has the possibility to know and verify the quality, the contents and the effectiveness of his own communication.

XVIII

Historical perspective sheds new light on most recent Catechism

Ana Ofelia Fernández
Servidora

The *Catechism* and salvation history

The *Catechism of the Catholic Church* is meant to be an instrument for the transmission of the content of the Christian faith. Accordingly, its roots are planted in the history of salvation: thus every one of its parts draws nourishment from Jesus Christ, the center of this history: "What was from the beginning, . . . we proclaim now to you" (Jn 1: 1-3).

It is the proclamation of the Son, of the only-begotten Son, who "can lead us to the love of the Father in the Spirit and make us sharers in the life of the Holy Trinity" (*Catechesi Tradendæ*, n. 5).

It is the Good News that joins time to eternity: "God has visited his people, he has fulfilled the promises made to Abraham and to his posterity . . ." (n. 422).

The "Amen" which closes the First Part (nn. 1061-1065), the "farewell" of the Second (n. 1690), the "I wish to see God" of the Third (nn. 2548-2550) and the "final doxology" of the Fourth (nn. 2855-2856) synthesize the entire eschatological conviction which is the driving force behind our earthly journey toward the eternal goal: the mysterious course we follow together with the Lord of history.

The *Catechism* and Church history

In the whole *Catechism* we find the teachings "of Sacred Scripture, the living Tradition of the Church and the authentic Magisterium", formulated with expressions which "the Holy Spirit has intimated to his Church" (Apostolic Constitution *Fidei Depositum*, n. 3), and which have been coined throughout the ages by the concrete *hic et nunc*.

In the themes, in the sources of inspiration, in the citations and in the references, one can see the Church, which recognizes "her origin in the plan of the Blessed Trinity and her progressive realization in history" (n. 758).

And like the Church herself, this new tool, the *Catechism*, "is in history, but at the same time transcends it" (n. 770). It draws its content from Revelation and delivers it today, with all the richness of an understanding deepened through the centuries. With the *chiaroscuro* of what is perceptible and is mystery, in the pages of our book the history of the Church is a great fresco, which arouses our admiration by its imposing totality and by the variety of its nuances (cf. n. 814). In it appear the dynamism of every Christian epoch and of every Christian place, the catholicity of the East and the West, the singular creativity of those who have handed down to us a greater and deeper understanding of the mystery and the experience of faith. We are introduced to the whole People of God, the bearer of the *sensus fidei* throughout the centuries (cf. nn. 871-873; 889), with its prototypes at the head: "the spiritual heritage of the Fathers and the Church's saints" (*Fidei Depositum*, n. 3).

By putting us in contact with the *history of the Church* and her 2,000 years of effective teaching in continuation of the instructive tradition of the Old Testament, the *Catechism* makes us appreciate the profound link between all the eras, agents and witnesses of the building up of the Body of Christ (cf. n. 789 ff.).

The *Catechism* and contemporary world history

Already in the title of the first chapter of Part I: "Man is 'capable' of God", we find a clear reference to our *contemporary history* which, restless and suffering as a result of immanentism, seeks with difficulty the way to the truth but, at the same time, in many different ways expresses the desire and search for God.

The *Catechism* does not regard itself as parallel to today's world: it was conceived in the time in which we live. The Pope called it the "post-conciliar *Catechism*" (Homily of Dec. 8, 1992), and we know well how Vatican II motivated the Church in the search for ways of being attuned to the contemporary world: "The Church is one, in her continuous encounter with the manifold realities which constitute the 'world of mankind' . . ." (John Paul II, Address to the Roman Curia, Dec. 22, 1992, n. 5). In their complex causes and effects and in today's network of sciences, technologies and ideologies involving all the areas of our life, these realities have culminated in causing current developments which are taking us almost by surprise. The close of the millennium enables us to perceive the beginning of a new synthesis, at least as an aspiration.

This whole problematic of the contemporary world is captured by the *Catechism* with the intuition and love of the Church, Mother and Teacher. She strives "calmly to show the strength and beauty of the doctrine of the faith" (*Fidei Depositum*, n. 1). By drawing forth this teaching from her rich deposit, she is able to illuminate our anxieties as people who are the products of "modernity".

This whole problematic of the contemporary world is captured by the *Catechism* with the intuition and love of the Church, Mother and Teacher. She strives "calmly to show the strength and beauty of the doctrine of the faith" (*Fidei Depositum*, n. 1). By drawing forth this teaching from her rich deposit, she is able to illuminate our anxieties as people who are the products of "modernity".

The *Catechism* and history of catechetics

The pedagogy of the Holy Father, who is always attentive to the human person and therefore to history, teaches us not to overlook anything in the present that is "history-making". With a vision that transcends the present moment, he enables us to see that with the *Catechism of the Catholic Church* we are confronted not just with any book, one of the many dealing with religious questions.

He tells us that the *Catechism* can be considered, in a certain sense and analogously, as the last document of Vatican II (cf. ibid., n. 3). For this reason, its *relevance* is evident (n. 11), as is its *continuity* with "the great tradition of the catechisms" of the Church (n. 13).

It is a historical constant that the great periods of renewal and creativity in the Church are always accompanied by a notable catechetical production (cf. nn. 8, 9, 10). These works and their authors do not form a monolithic body apart but, although often separated by centuries or by the particulars of space and of time, link up with one another, because they take up what is enduring in each.

These characteristics of *relevance* and *continuity* show once again the freedom with which the Church draws from the "new" and the "old" (cf. Mt 13: 52). The teachings of life which Deuteronomy gives us (4: 10; 11: 19), Jesus' own proclamation to the people (Mt 5: 2; 11: 1; Mk 1: 21-22; Jn 7: 14), the mandate to continue this mission (Mt 28: 19-20) unbroken from the time of the primitive Church (Acts 2: 42; 5: 21; 14: 21), the official catechetical literature of every era: all of this has made its contribution to the letter or the spirit of the present *Catechism*.

We can understand the *Catechism of the Catholic Church* better if we re-read the various catechisms drawn up through-out the centuries, seeking to reach the central core of each and not a reductive theoretical outline. We will discover in their pages the vitality that made them suitable for their time and for those to whom they were addressed, who, in turn were able to use them as tools: as means, not an end.

In those first programmatic lines or writings, such as the *Didaché, De catechizandis rudibus* and so many others (cf. *Catechesi Tradendæ*, n. 12), appear the first rough outlines of this genre, which will progressively take shape, on the one hand, in actual works under various names, such as: inter-rogations, elucidations, septenaries, sermons . . ., catechisms (the first to be called such is the *Catechism of York* [1357]); on the other hand, in texts which do not constitute autonomous books but which form part of some synodal legislation, such as the first canon of the Synod of Lavaur (1368) or the one the Council of Tortosa (1429) ordered to be written.

This brief article cannot review the entire catechetical evolution of the Church. However, I think it would be well to dwell, if only in overview, on a moment and an aspect which are "key" for catechetics and which can help us better understand our *Catechism* through history, in this case that of the 16th century. We will thus gain a clearer insight into the source of the present Catechism's structure, as well as into how a *Catechism* destined for the whole Church can serve as a "reference point" for the particular Churches.

A fundamental moment: the Council of Trent

In order to trace the span of the modern age in the Church, (without wishing to mark initial lines or static partitions), we can legitimately consider an event that was central: the Council of Trent (1545-1563). This assembly responded to the call for reform *in capites* and *in membris* which was being heard with some insistence.

The Fathers of Trent singled out, as a top priority, the solid formation of parish priests in order to cultivate a strong faith among the people who were suffering as a result of ignorance and the massive spread of doctrines which deviated from the Roman Magisterium.

Luther and other reformers were popularizing catechetical books—enchiridion, catechisms—which were spreading with greater ease because Christians were not prepared to understand that in the very structure of these works the contents of the faith were being changed. The new theses on justification had an impact on people's vision of the sacraments and undermined the bases of morality, which was thus being transformed into a formal code of duties. Luther preserved the four parts which formed the outline of a catechism, but gave this outline a new order in accordance with his new theological conception:

- Commandments;
- Creed;
- Prayer;
- Baptism and the Lord's Supper.

When the Council of Trent ordered the writing of the *Catechism*, which was destined *ad parochos* and was completed under Saint Pius V in 1566, it was organized in the light of the theological-catechetical structure it was to uphold. It turned out to be so solid and suitable to the catechetical "edifice", that it has been an effective model for a good 400 years. And even today, the four pillars of the *Roman Catechism*:

- Creed;
- Sacraments;
- Commandments;
- Prayer form the very structural basis upon which is built the new edifice which the *Catechism of the Catholic Church* has designed for modern man.

The Apostolic Constitution *Fidei Depositum* explicitly acknowledges the fact that the articulation of its contents stems from the *Catechism* of Trent, and it brings out the interrelationship and the mutual influence of the four parts, thus demonstrating the unity of the new *Catechism*, founded on the "wondrous unity of the mystery of God" (cf. n. 3).

A fundamental aspect: creativity in unity

It is important to recognize the fact that the *Catechism 'ad parochos'* or the *Roman Catechism* did not impose uniformity on catechetics, nor did it turn it into something static. On the contrary, it is possible to show that it gave the impetus for a true phenomenon of catechetical creativity, which became even more notable and effective as a result of the great 16th-century expansion of ecclesial geography, which presented new peoples and cultures as a challenge to adaptation and to the creation of methods and tools for evangelization.

Regarding this flexibility of the *Catechism* of 1566 in relation to local catechisms, among the many and varied examples which could be cited, I choose one, namely that of Latin America, which is a particularly eloquent case. *Mutatis mutandis*, the study of this example can be a source of inspiration for the inculturation of the present *Catechism*.

I am speaking of the *Catechism* of the Third Provincial Council of Lima (1582-83). The Lima Synod had it drawn up because of the great need to give suitable tools to missionaries because of the proliferation of improvised manuals which were not helping to consolidate the faith of the local inhabitants of the Peruvian area. It arose in response to a local need, but it was done also, as the Preface says, "to be something very much in conformity with what the Sacred Council of Trent recommends regarding doctrine."

In a brief sentence those Synodal Fathers explained what line they would follow, showing the convergence between fidelity to the Magisterium and freedom of inculturation. In fact they asked the writers "with regard to the substance and the order, to follow as closely as possible the '*Catechism* of Pius V of revered memory" and with regard to the manner and to the style to seek to attain the greatest progress of the Indios, as is observed by the same '*Catechism* of the Supreme Pontiff, . . ." (cf. *Doctrina y Catecismo para instruccion de los indios* . . .. Lima, 1584).

With the exemplary realism of Pastors, then, the Bishops of the Council of Lima took the *Roman Catechism* as a reference point They conformed to it in the "substance", that is, in the contents, which they presented in a flexible way, so as to shed light on the themes proper to their particular audience; and in the "order", inasmuch as this has an intimate connection with that content.

The methodology, on the other hand, was conceived totally in reference to the local customs, with the intention of making the text an effective tool, as in fact it turned out to be. Accordingly, the Lima *Catechism* was trilingual (Spanish, Quechua and Aymara) and, in the development of the topics and in the levels, different approaches were taken in various books, according to the anthropological-cultural situation and the degree of stability which Christianity had reached at the time.

From the history of catechetics this aspect of creativity in unity is another of: the services towards which the *Catechism* urges us.

Two statements of John Paul II, taken from the speech in which he introduced the *Catechism of the Catholic Church* (December 7, 1992), can inspire our further reflection on this work in relation to history.

The first of these statements views the Catechism's transcendence with respect to today: "The publication of the text must certainly be counted among the major events of the Church's recent history" (n. 4).

The second refers to the source, in time, of this contemporary centrality: " . . . In it we have a convergence and collection in a harmonious synthesis of the Church's past, with her tradition, her history of listening, proclaiming, celebrating and witnessing the word, with her Councils, doctors and saints. Thus through successive generations, resounds the enduring and ever timely, evangelical Magisterium of Christ, light of mankind for 20 centuries."

In Church history, 1992 will be the year of the *Catechism*, and it is not an isolated historical event: it is inserted within the great events of the present "turning point" which, in order to go all the way, needs tools which can help it to become rooted in transcendence. History starts with a "today". This "today of 1992" has given us a work which, as it goes on its way, will continue to develop its potential for illuminating the faith of mankind in the third millennium.

XIX

The new Roman Catechism compared to the 'Roman Catechism' of Trent

Fr. Raúl Lanzetti
Roman Athenæum of the Holy Cross

It is still too early to offer a precise evaluation of the similarities and differences between these two great Catholic catechetical texts. It is possible, however, to dwell on some aspects that at first glance are more evident and more greatly appreciable.

A comparison of their respective origins

The need for compiling a catechism for the whole Church was pointed out during different periods of the Council of Trent. However, the concrete decision on this proposal was made only in the last stage. It was within one of the conciliar commissions that the imperial legate, Archbishop Anton Brus von Müglitz of Pécs, Hungary, suggested the compilation of a conciliar *Catechism* (obviously universal). The general consensus which had been growing until that time then took a more precise direction.

Later a team of theologians was formed; under the direction of Cardinal Girolamo Seripando, one of the papal legates, it would concern itself with drawing up a project to be presented later to the Council. Theologians of the most important universities worked on the drafting. Diocesan priests and those of the major religious orders were present. Meanwhile a decision was formally made by the Council to draw up a catechism for parish priests (canon *Ut Fidelis*). The sudden interruption of the Council caused the suspension of work on the document and the task was transferred to the Holy See (Decree *Sacrosancta*).

Unlike the *Roman Catechism*, the present *Catechism of the Catholic Church* did not explicitly originate in the Council. In spite of this it should be noted that there is a coincidence in its synodal origin since it was the second Extraordinary Synod that decided to ask the Apostolic See to draft a catechism for the universal Church.

It is however important to consider the current Catechism's various connections with Vatican II. First of all it is a fact that the initiative came to maturity through the progressive knowledge and application of Vatican II; it was also desired as an additional pastoral tool in applying the Council to the real life of the whole Church. Therefore, although the origin of the *Catechism of the Catholic Church* is not found in the documents of the Council, it is certainly to be found in the desire to apply them.

Furthermore, the special character of the second Extraordinary Synod should not be overlooked. Celebrated 20 years after Vatican II, it examined all that had been done in the intervening period. Therefore, from this point of view the reference to Vatican II was a preamble to collegial reflection on the future *Catechism*. Furthermore, this pastoral initiative did not emerge from a partisan consideration of the Council but arose in the context of a total evaluation of its understanding and application within the Church.

On the other hand, the Apostolic See's responsibility in drawing up the *Catechism of the Catholic Church* should be pointed out. In the case of the *Roman Catechism*, the transfer of the task to the Holy See was accidental. For the present *Catechism*, however, the Holy See's involvement was desired from the very start.

The drafting, approval and publication of the text

In regard to the editing of the *Roman Catechism*, the overall direction was the responsibility of Saint Charles Borromeo, the Cardinal Nephew of Pope Pius IV. Four important members of the final Tridentine period worked on it: Archbishop Muzio Calini of Zara, Archbishop Leonardo De Marini, O.P. of Lanciano, and Bishop Egidio Foscarari, O.P. of Modena. The secretary was Francisco Foreiro, O.P., preacher at the Court of Portugal. The definitive Latin edition was the work of the humanist Giulio Poggiano.

Later revisions were mostly the work of some experts of the Vatican Apostolic Library, namely: Cardinal Guglielmo Sirleto and Mons. Mariano Vittori. Nearly 2,000 suggested emendations have been found. The most important part of their work consisted in revising biblical, patristic and magisterial quotations.

One clear similarity between the *Catechism of the Catholic Church* and the *Roman Catechism* is that their drafters were diocesan Bishops. The editorial process differs however due to the vast consultation with the Episcopate during the revision of the present *Catechism* (more than 20,000 proposed emendations, 10 times more than those proposed for the Tridentine *Catechism*). Both facts point to the *Catechism of the Catholic Church*'s strong roots in episcopal collegiality. This pastoral initiative sprang from and developed in the *affectus collegialis*.

As for the *approval and publication* of the *Roman Catechism*, it should be noted that, in actual fact, its editing was already finished under Pius IV. However, the approval of the text fell to his successor, Saint Pius V. Guglielmo Sirleto and Leonardo De Marini—witnesses of the previous history of the text participated in the final phase of the work, as did Tommaso Manrique O.P., Master of the Sacred Palace (today Theologian of the Pontifical Household), and apparently Eustachio Locatelli O.P., Procurator General of the Dominicans. Saint Pius V approved the text presented to him, making only some observations of a formal nature. The text was printed at the *Stamperia del Popolo Romano* by Paolo Manuzio, in three first editions: in folio Latin (*editio princeps*), 8vo Latin and 8vo Italian. Other translations (German, Polish and French) were printed in subsequent years.

The most significant fact in this regard is the manner chosen for publication. In the case of the *Roman Catechism*, Pope Pius V's *Motu Proprio Pastorali Officio* was simply the editorial privilege conferred on Manuzio. As a matter of interest here, the text was limited to describing what the Council of Trent had desired, and was then carried out in Rome in accordance with the Council's wish. There was no expression of the special involvement of the supreme authority to stress the text's authoritativeness. For the *Catechism of the Catholic Church* the system worked quite differently. It is already rather significant that a degree of publicity was given to the papal approval (June 25, 1992). It is even more so that the Holy Father had it promulgated with an Apostolic Constitution (*Fidei Depositum*, October 11, 1992). This fact is in itself sufficiently eloquent to express the authoritativeness accorded it.

To all this must be added the various ceremonies and celebrative events for its presentation. It is a matter of conjecture as to when the *Roman Catechism* emerged from Manuzio's printery, but it must have been during the latter half of September 1566. On the contrary, the release of the *Catechism of the Catholic Church* was marked by a triduum of official celebrations, indicating the importance attached to this event.

Comparison of some technical characteristics

Both Catechisms belong to the *maior* catechetical literature in that they are not directly addressed to the faithful (children or adults), but seek to inspire the entire ministry of the word, which is the concern of pastors.

Then, in the case of the *Roman Catechism*, there is ample correspondence with the pre-Tridentine catechetical literature (Carranza, Gropper, Nausea and Hosius). In the *Catechism of the Catholic Church*, although the consultation of catechisms written after Vatican II can be seen, the influence of contemporary catechetical works is far less evident than in the case of the old *Roman Catechism*. In fact, in order to be universal, a catechism must now be open to the ritual, theological, spiritual and disciplinary multiformity present in the richness of Catholicism. Therefore it cannot remain tied to works that are closer to certain ecclesial and social contexts. In the 1500's, on the other hand, the Church was mainly central and western European and therefore the pastoral choices of the "Old World" were given priority.

In both Catechisms, the form of exposition is fully *catechetical* inasmuch as the discussion does not proceed according to the patterns of professional theology (dialectical/probative), but is expressed in a language of simple statement and ecclesial meditation on revealed truth. The basic outline is of the type used to *comment on and explain texts*. In fact, it should not be forgotten that three of the four parts are true texts in themselves, namely, the Apostles' Creed, the Decalogue and the Lord's Prayer. Furthermore, the last two are biblical texts. In this way catechesis appears as a formulation of the way in which the Church understands these texts. Therefore an explanation is developed which constantly refers to the Fathers, the liturgy and the Magisterium of the Church. Together with these fundamental contents, there are others which either serve as an introduction, as a parallel or successive development of a topic, or as a practical conclusion for application to daily life.

However some important differences should be pointed out:

- although the present *Catechism* is indebted to all the progress made to date in the critical-literary field (although not explicitly), it does not overload the text with technical details;

- above all other parts are much more developed, particularly the *first sections* which lay the foundation for the various other parts.

As regards the formal arrangement, in the *Roman Catechism* the topics developed are clear and precise. However, this is not evident from a reading of the content because the typographical layout was imperfect, and not only according to modern criteria. With the *Catechism of the Catholic Church* greater attention was paid to the text's formal structure. In fact this is outlined in almost minute detail, from the parts and chapters to the correlative system of numbering the individual paragraphs, passing through other intermediate divisions. This method will greatly facilitate the reading of the text.

Pastoral motives

Roughly, it may be said that the *Roman Catechism* gave an official stamp to the renewal process begun by the *Catholic reformation* of the pre-Tridentine period (the first half of the

1500's). The problem that was faced was the secularization of central and western Europe through *religious formalism.* Christianity was being reduced to merely external practices (ceremonies and social customs) divesting it of its Christian essence. The Catholic reform was intended to reconstitute *Christian authenticity* from within. An important priority was therefore given to catechesis. It was structured around the three theological virtues, according to the model of Saint Augustine. Being Christian cannot be reduced to a name and ceremonies, but first of all means to be a *believer and lover in hope.*

On the other hand, the *Roman Catechism* had to apply appropriate *discernment* with regard to the Protestant reform. In the Protestant view, *rituals*—especially the sacraments—were useless and good works impossible, since the inner justification of the Christian was likewise impossible. These views were in clear contrast with the Catholic reform (to be distinguished from the Counterreformation, which followed the Council of Trent), causing bitter controversy between the two trends.

The *Roman Catechism* kept its distance from the strongly polemical style of the previous dispute. In fact it never names Luther and the other Protestant reformers. Its authors prefer to state impartially what the Church believes. Above all the plan of the different parts of the *Catechism* reflects this desire for discernment in regard to Protestantism. Being a Christian is based on *grace,* the gift of God, which comes to us through *faith* (Part I = Creed) and the *sacraments* (Part II); then, once interiorly reborn and reconstituted through this gift, we can give life to *works* (Part III = Decalogue) and to *prayer* (Part IV = the Lord's Prayer).

It may be said that there is continuity between the present *Catechism* and the *Roman Catechism* in their goal of evangelization and the recovery of interiority mentioned previously. Hence there is also a similarity in the general plan of the work with its four characteristic parts: dogma (Creed), liturgy, morals (Decalogue) and prayer. However, the analogy between the present *Catechism* and the old *Roman Catechism* should be seen in broader terms. Obviously, today one cannot express oneself in the same way as was done 400 years ago: circumstances have changed and theological knowledge of Revelation has progressed.

As for its doctrinal discernment, the *Catechism of the Catholic Church* does not have to face a particular emergency on a doctrinal and moral level, as the *Roman Catechism* had to in relation to Protestantism. The present *Catechism* tends to place emphasis on the positive aspect of the necessary *communio in fide*. As Vatican II teaches, the Church's missionary strength is rooted in her own internal unity. Only a Church that is truly one can give life to a unifying mission in the heart of contemporary mankind; and this missionary communion is rooted in the *unity of faith*.

In this sense it was necessary to show the internal cohesiveness of the Church's faith; it is a unity, and not a collection of more or less scattered religious convictions. On the other hand, also at stake is the necessary communion in faith between Catholic Christians. The many ways of expressing the faith can only apply to its accidental aspects. The substance is always one and the same. Therefore, due to the phenomenon of the current subjectivism which is at the basis of the so-called "partial identification" with the Church, an authoritative clarification in this regard was extremely necessary.

On the other hand, both Catechisms were conceived as *pastoral tools for a changing era* in the life of the Church, because of their respective links with the Ecumenical Councils from which they derive. The *Roman Catechism* contributed to the transition from the crisis of late medieval Christianity to the ecclesial and missionary revival that took place after the Council of Trent. For its part, Vatican II also brought about important renewal in the lives of the People of God. In that sense, the present *Catechism* seeks to root that renewal more firmly in the Church as she approaches the Third Millennium, thus marking her daily exercise of the ministry of the word.

XX

New Catechism presents essential elements of papal social teaching

Fr. Albert Chapelle, S.J.

"The *Catechism* will include 'new things and old' (cf. Mt 13: 52), since the faith is always the same and yet the source of ever new lights" (John Paul II, *Fidei Depositum*). The Church believes that she has received from divine Revelation whatever is necessary to "respond to the questions of our time" (ibid.). A person's moral concern accompanies the growth of his powers. Not even the greatest mastery over the earth can assure man of a better morality; as his powers unfold, this mastery creates new seductions, more unavoidable questions, more lethal temptations.

Economic development linked to the industrial revolution has forced the moral conscience and the ecclesial Magisterium to define the exigencies of social justice. The "social question" has been the occasion for an intense papal and conciliar teaching since the last century. The essential elements of this teaching are found in the *Catechism* regarding the human community (1877-1948) and within the framework of the seventh commandment (nn. 2401-2463). Today, it is between nations that "the inequality of resources and of economic means" is causing a veritable gap as well as posing terrifying threats (n. 2437-2442). "The acceptance by human society of conditions of human misery that lead to death without any effort to bring relief is a scandalous injustice and a grave fault. Those in business who employ usury and commercial practices that cause the hunger and death of their brothers in humanity, indirectly commit murder; they must answer for this" (n. 2269). And it cites Amos 8: 4-10. It could well have cited also the texts of *Populorum Progressio, Sollicitudo Rei Socialis*and *Centesimus Annus.*

Terrible as these problems may be, other equally grave threats have a still more direct bearing on the *physical* life of the human being. The accumulation of knowledge and power reveals in a startling way the violence latent in man. This has been the case from the beginning and since the days of Cain. Institutions of political reason, scientific conquests and technical achievements are instrumentalized by lethal violence which, in a way that defies reason, turns man into the worst enemy of man. The totalitarian regimes and the world wars of the 20th century, the arms race and innumerable armed conflicts have not sufficed to quench a thirst for violence which socialization does not appease, but rather increases. The fifth commandment, "You shall not kill" (Ex 20: 13), is violated as a matter of course. Its exposure touches the nerve of political life and of the contemporary moral conscience. *Abortion* (nn. 2270-2275) and *euthanasia* (nn. 2276-2279) have become political problems; the *death penalty* (nn. 2265-2267) and the *"just war"* (nn. 2307-2317) constitute ever more decisive moral challenges.

Human right to life is inalienable

Medically assisted procreation (nn. 2376-2377) constitutes another area of social and financial, political and moral debate. They are closely associated with the status of the human being from the moment of conception. Their development and their moral evaluation presuppose a unique understanding of human reproduction and human sexuality. According to the Instruction *Donum Vitæ* (1987), their moral evaluation is related to the gift of love and the gift of life, to the sacred character of human life from its very origin, and to the integrity of the human body. These technologies, as well as the research or scientific experimentation on the human being (nn. 2292-2293) and organ transplants (n. 2296) pose the greatest problems to contemporary society.

These fearful questions compromise the human body and respect for human life "from its beginning to its term" (n.

2258). *Abortion*(nn. 2270-2275) and *euthanasia*(nn. 2276-2279) constitute frightful, but obligatory themes for contemporary moral reflection. Professor Michel Schooyans of Louvain -La-Neuve has drawn attention to the "totalitarian drift" which threatens the physical destruction of societies seduced by scientistic and liberal ideologies.[1] But "the right to life and to the physical integrity of every human being from conception until death" (n. 2273) is inalienable because "the human person has been willed for himself in the image and likeness of the living and holy God" (n. 2319).

This fundamental right of the human person must be recognized and respected in a state of law "as a constitutive element of civil society and of its legislation" (n. 2273); Whether it is a matter of human beings just conceived or on the point of dying, once "a positive law has deprived a category of human beings from the protection which civil legislation ought to accord them, the State has in principle denied the equality of all before the law" (n. 2273). A democratic and pluralistic society does not always recognize the demands of moral reason; it is nevertheless juridically obligated to respect the fundamental rights of individuals, the constitutive elements of a state of law and the elementary principles of political reason. This is the duty of civil authorities (n. 2235). Public authorities are to be held accountable for it (n. 2237).

The legalization of induced abortion (as well as of *euthanasia*) and its inevitable consequences of research on embryos, the freezing of the same, their production and their exploitation "as disposable biological material" (n. 2275), constitute major political errors. At the same time they are concessions to violence, offenses against law and injustices against persons.

The teachings of the *Catechism* on the *death penalty* (nn. 2265-2267) and the *just war*(nn. 2307-2317) fall neatly within the teaching on the prohibition of murder.

"The murder of a human being is gravely contrary to the dignity of the person and to the sanctity of the Creator" (n. 2320). The moral law proscribes the voluntary killing of an innocent human being, that is to say, of an innocent man, one who is not harming anyone, is not at present inflicting damage on individuals and on society. This law is "universally valid: it is binding for each and every one, always and everywhere" (n. 2261).

"The legitimate defense of individuals and of societies does not constitute an exception to the prohibition of murder" (n. 2263), because "the act of self-defense can entail a double effect: one is the preservation of one's own life, the other the death of the aggressor. . . .. Only the first is willed; the other is not" (n. 2263). "One who defends his life is not guilty of homicide even if he is compelled to deal his attacker a mortal blow" (n. 2264). It is the same with societies as with individuals: their defense "can be not only a right, but even a serious duty" for one who is in a position of responsibility (n. 2265).

Right to collective defense based on common good

A few doctrinal presuppositions should here be stressed:

- There are no exceptions to the prohibition of murder.
- Violence is congenitally present in human beings and their societies since "the first sin of man" (n. 397). This "inclination to evil and to death" (n. 403; cf. n. 407) is one of the consequences for humanity (n. 402) of the sin of Adam. "Insofar as men are sinners, the threat of war hangs over them and will so continue until the coming of Christ" (n. 2317, citing *Gaudium et Spes,* n. 78, 4).
- It is the obligation of the political authorities (nn. 1897-1904) to contain violence, to assure the common good of the community and hence respect for persons (nn. 1907, 2237), social well-being (n. 1908) and ultimately peace (n. 1909). The common good "is the basis of the right to legitimate personal and collective defense" (n. 1909).

These moral principles ensure the right and the duty of public authorities to defend the lives of individuals in a violent world, the "common good of the family or of the community" (n. 2265). They proscribe the exercise to this effect of a "disproportionate violence" (n. 2264): this would amount to a deviation of the intention and a perversion of the will. The doctrine thus confirms "the permanent validity of the moral law during armed conflicts"

(n. 2312, *Gaudium et Spes*, n. 79, 4). But "to preserve the common good of society requires that the aggressor be rendered harmless" (n. 2266). For this reason, "those in authority have the right to use weapons to repel aggressors from the civil community for which they are responsible" (n. 2266).

"Each citizen and government is obliged to work to avoid war" (n. 2308; cf. *Gaudium et Spes*, nn. 79-82). If other than military operations "suffice to defend human lives against the aggressor" and to protect the public peace, these non-violent measures are to be preferred because they are more proportionate and "more conformed to the end desired and to human dignity" (n. 2267). One ought then "to consider rigorously the precise conditions for legitimate defense by military force. The gravity of such a decision makes it subject to rigorous conditions of moral legitimacy" (n. 2309). "These are the traditional elements enumerated in the doctrine of the 'just war'" (n. 2304), as well as of armed resistance to oppression inflicted by a political power (cf. n. 2243).

The Church recalls the beatitude of the "peacemakers" (n. 2330); she prays to the Lord that he deliver us "from famine, from plague and from war" (n. 2327). She also assumes the task of illumining the human mind with the light of Revelation so that it can confront violence as well as its obligation to contain it. War is not justified by the right to reparation or compensation. Only "the neutralizing of the aggressor" (n. 2266) can legitimize the defense of nations by the use of arms.

The same goes for the *death penalty*. The prohibition of murder is inviolable. Violence reigns in society. It is by "title" of legitimate defense that holders of public authority are said to have "the right and the duty to administer proportionate punishment . . . not excluding . . . the *death penalty*" (n. 2266).

The *Catechism* acknowledges and recalls the teachings of Pius XII and of Paul VI on the *death penalty*.[2] In conformity with the doctrine on authority (nn. 1897-1904), the common good (nn. 1905-1912) and the duties of the public authorities in civil society (nn. 2234-2243), the punishment inflicted by courts counterbalances the disorder; it has an "expiatory value", it should also "preserve public order" and finally "contribute to the correction of the criminal" (n. 2266).

"Penal law is one of the means by which the State endeavors to protect organized social life", said Pius XII in 1957. "To preserve the common good of society requires that the aggressor be rendered harmless. It is by this title of legitimate defense that the traditional teaching of the Church has recognized the legitimacy of the right and duty of the legitimate public authority to inflict penalties proportionate to the gravity of the crime without excluding the *death penalty* in cases of extreme gravity" (n. 2266). In fact the Fourth Lateran Council acknowledged that the secular power "could exercise a judgment of blood without mortal sin, on condition that it is acting . . . not with hatred but with justice, not with thoughtlessness but after deliberation *(consulte)*"(DS 795; D 425).

The Episcopal Conferences of several Western countries have in recent years made a prudential judgment on this matter.[3] In their estimation, the conditions are no longer such that a judge of a democratic nation and of a *constitutional State* can still morally inflict the *death penalty* in peacetime. The *Catechism* supports these authorized declarations by a moral claim: "If (in fact) non-bloody means adequately defend human lives from the aggressor and protect public order and the security of individuals, the authorities will confine themselves to these means, because they correspond better to the concrete conditions of the common good and are more in line with the dignity of the human person" (n. 2267).

Many people, Christians and non Christians alike, have struggled and if necessary still fight for the abolition of the *death penalty*. The *Catechism* brings to this political struggle a precise moral argument. It does not denounce as erroneous or culpable the public powers which consider the *death penalty* indispensable to the legitimate defense of individuals and societies. But it condemns the cruel punishments "commonly practiced by legitimate governments", such as torture (n. 2298). It rigorously enunciates the strict conditions of a possibly legitimate defense of the *death penalty*. Moral and political education is working to make this bloody procedure no longer necessary for disarming an aggressor. In the terms of St. Thomas Aquinas, as we have said, "It is illicit to exercise greater violence than is necessary" (n. 2264). This does not amount to judging a moral act according to the proportion of its effects; it only means not considering as voluntary homicide the legitimate defense of society by public authority; it means urging the political powers to limit themselves to minimal coercive measures in order "to defend human lives from the aggressor and to protect public order and the security of individuals" (n. 2267).

To give and accept life means to love

The *just war* and the *death penalty* remain signs of violence and of the evil that is still at work in human history and always will be. The Lord conquered hatred, at the very moment when "he did not defend himself" (n. 2262). It is to its shame and confusion that humanity confesses its violence and implores the forgiveness of God. The massacred innocents remain among humanity the witnesses to its Savior. The honor of the soldier and the dignity of the judge reside in their modesty. To receive and to give back life, from conception to death is to love; to take life away or to remove it is hatred. To give life and to preserve it belongs to God; to defend it is the task of man.

NOTES

1   M. Schooyans, *La dérive totalitaire du libéralisme,* Éditions universitaires, Paris, 1991.
2   Four instructions of Pius XII can be mentioned here: *Address to the Sixth International Congress of Penal Law* on 5 October 1953 (*AAS* XLV, 1953, p. 730); *Speech to the Italian Catholic Jurists* on 5 October 1954 (*AAS* XLVII, 1955, p. 60) and 5 February 1955 (ibid., p. 72); and finally, *Address to a Group of Italian Jurists* on 25 May 1957 (*AAS* XLIX, 1957, p. 403). We cite from this last text: "Your association bears the title . . . 'Friends of Prisoners'. But the convicted who need assistance are not only those in prison. The penal justice of the past, that of the present and, to a certain extent, that of the future as well— if it is true that in many ways history teaches what will happen in the future—has known

or will know penalties of physical torture, mutilations, deaths and capital punishment under various forms." Pius XII does not make a moral judgment on these "penalties". The latter are considered as measures taken by public authority with regard to the culpable who have violated the law in force, by means of which the State must protect organized social existence. The Pope affirmed: "Punishment can be considered as a function both of human law and of divine law, but . . . the juridical aspect is never a purely abstract conception, entirely isolated from any relationship with the moral aspect." And finally, the Pope recalls: "between the inexorable demand for satisfaction and the inevitable punishment, God has himself inserted his mercy in the redemptive work of his Son" *(Documentation Catholique,* 1254, 23 June 1957, col. 773-782).

3   Thus the Bishops of Canada, on 26 January 1973 *(Documentation Catholique,* 1627 [1973] 246) and on 4 March 1976 *(Documentation Catholique,* 1694 [1976] 277). Likewise, the Justice and Peace Commissions of Ireland on 11 November 1976 *(Documentation Catholique,* 1710 [1976] 1081) and of the United States on 9 December 1976 *(Documentation Catholique,* 1713 [1977] 139-140). Finally the permanent Council of the French Episcopate on 11 January 1977 *(Documentation Catholique,* 1713 [1977] 147).

XXI

Man and woman are loved by the Lord and desired for one another

Anna Maria Cànopi, O.S.B.
Mater Ecclesiæ Abbey, Isola S. Giulio

A mature fruit of Vatican II, the *Catechism of the Catholic Church* represents a synthesis of the Church's perennial teaching, drawn up also with consideration for the different cultures and developments of human history, a dizzying change during this last part of the 20th century, so full of important events and changes at the world level. Each rapid change in our way of thinking is often accompanied by a practical relativism manifest in an arbitrary, permissive way of living. Christians, too, risk becoming accustomed to a certain worldly mentality and to letting themselves be guided by subjective opinions rather than by the sense of the true faith.

For this reason the *Catechism* devotes great attention to the Christian concept of the person and to interpersonal relationships; because there is a tense conflict between the two sexes in modern society, it does not fail to specify the basic points regarding this matter. It would, however, be too much to expect the *Catechism* to treat this "problem" in detail. As is the case for other subjects regarding the human person—male and female—the concept emerging from the *Catechism* is what the Church has always affirmed in the light of the Scriptures and Tradition, and filtered through the various cultures of the peoples being evangelized.

It should be noted, however, that the ambiguity and lack of scruples of modern culture, characterized as it is by an unrestrained search for autonomy and selfish gratification of the instinct for possession and pleasure, has effects which appear to be extremely harmful, especially to women.

The models of woman as held up and proposed by the mass media are often so erroneous and disconcerting as to reduce woman to a mere consumer product and, at the same time, to a poisoned food as it were which destroys whoever consumes it. If it is true that the shameful "marketing" of woman can be traced back to remote times, it is also true that the mystery of sin is developing in an ever more refined and unforseeable manner.

The exploitation of woman, as happens nowadays, is a mortal blow to the heart of all humanity. This can be observed at every level (familial, professional political and social); therefore there is increasing interest in woman's identity and role in the Church and in human society as we are about to begin the third millennium of the Christian era in ever more dramatic living conditions.

Woman in the design of creation

Sometimes explicitly and again implicitly, the *Catechism* first presents the face of the "eternal woman", conceived and desired by God as an image of his loving devotion, together with man, her partner: "Man and woman are *created*, that is *desired by God:* perfectly equal in one way, inasmuch as they are human beings, and in the other way, in their respective identities as male and female. 'To be man' or 'to be woman' is a reality that is good and desired by God" (n. 369).

From this comes "the insuppressible and identical dignity" that man and woman possess in the eyes of their Creator and which they must recognize in one another. Both "reflect the wisdom and goodness of the Creator", both are loved by God, and are "desired by God for one another" (n. 371), i.e., placed in a relationship of love. In this enrapturing reciprocity woman is particularly characterized by her oblatory nature, as being a gift and source of consolation and joy for the other. She, in fact, "draws from man a cry of admiration, an exclamation of love and communion" because man "discovers woman as another 'I' of the same humanity" (cf. n. 371). Since each is complete in him or herself and open to communion, they help and enrich one another precisely because of their differences (cf. n. 372) and in the measure in which each one authentically lives his or her own specific nature. With this clear statement, we see the failure of all the vague reasons for seeking equality of the sexes based on the presumed rights of the woman to "act like a man", that is, to assume typically male roles while renouncing her own; while, on the contrary, "the harmony of the human couple and of society depends in part on the way in which complementarity, mutual need and reciprocal help are lived between the sexes" (cf. nn. 2333; 2433).

Unfortunately from its beginnings the wonderful harmony of God's creative plan suffered the tragic consequences of sin (cf. n. 400); a confusion of instincts caused a tension in the man-woman relationship, a tension which seems to be insuperable, a tension which often results in the most difficult and humiliating consequences for woman.

This is not because she was more responsible for the fall but because, due to her delicate biological and psychological structure, she is more vulnerable. This does not however imply a condition of inferiority. The *Catechism* emphasizes the fact that, just as the temptation of the evil one came through a woman, so too the priceless grace of redemption also came through a woman. In the *Protoevangelium* (Gn 3: 15) a battle between "the serpent and the woman" is foretold, one in which her descendants will be victorious. The reference is to Mary, whom God chose and planned as the "new Eve", true mother of the living, our mother in the order of grace, the mother, that is, of mankind reborn in Christ, victorious over sin and death (cf. nn. 410-411).

Woman in the plan of redemption

Before Mary and approaching her over the centuries, woman had partially regained her dignity through physical and spiritual motherhood, and she had already enlightened and sustained the journey of human generations. The "holy women" of the people of the old covenant—Sarah, Rebecca, Rachel, Miriam, Deborah, Hanna, Judith, Esther—in fact "kept the hope of the salvation of Israel alive" (cf. n. 64). He who was "born of woman", of the integral woman, all beautiful in the order of grace, was in a certain way conceived and borne in the womb by "many other women" who, by their generous dedication in service to life, had helped to prepare the new times (cf. n. 489).

Last of all, in the fullness of time, Jesus himself, while choosing men to be his Apostles on whom he would found his Church, does not deprive himself of the help of the female element (cf. Lk 8: 1-3); rather he stresses its irreplaceable value, proposing it as the example of faith, constancy and total devotion (cf. Mt 9: 20-22; 15: 21-28; 26: 6-13; Lk 10: 38-42; 18: 1-5; 21: 1-4; etc.).

It was the women who, together with Mary, the mother of Jesus, had the courage to follow Christ as far as Calvary and to remain steadfast at his cross and his tomb with that intense empathy which makes them capable of living and dying in others. They thus had the privilege of being the first to see and announce the risen Christ: "Mary Magdalen and the holy women who were going to finish embalming Jesus' body . . . were the first to meet the risen Lord. The women were thus the first messengers of Christ's resurrection for the Apostles themselves" (n. 641).

In this wording the *Catechism* seems to stress this fact intentionally, as if to emphasize that one can see with the intuition of the heart—an essential prerogative of woman—before one can see with the senses and reason. For the same reason the "holy women"—and the *Catechism* notes this too with interest— together with Mary, the mother of Jesus, persevere in prayer where the disciples of the risen Lord are gathered to await Pentecost (cf. Acts 1: 12-14). Thus in a certain way they bear in their maternal womb the new People of God, the true Israel; they watch over its birth and they support its first steps (cf. n. 965).

It may not be excessive to state that woman has a certain connaturalness with the Holy Spirit because of her capacity to love, to welcome life and to give it. For this reason, in Mary she is placed at the source of regenerating grace. The Church is "feminine", as is the community of the redeemed incorporated into Christ its Head, mother and nurse of all those whom she generates in the Spirit. The feminine element has its own irreplaceable position in the economy of redemption because it expresses the tenderness of the merciful and patient God who suffers . . ..

The exclusion of women from the ordained priesthood, to which the *Catechism* soberly refers in n. 1577, should not be misunderstood as a limitation or, worse, as a discrimination, but rather as the acknowledgment of a different way of participating in the work of redemption with respect to the creative and redemptive design of God and the explicit will of Jesus Christ.

Beyond every question of a social and cultural nature, it is evident that the role of woman in the Church has always been essentially maternal and charismatic. For this reason, because of the original grace of which she is the bearer, woman can exercise a profound and beneficial spiritual influence on the ministry of the sacred hierarchy.

Woman in the family

The *Catechism*, for reasons that are more than justified, gives ample coverage to the sacrament of Marriage and the family. In this area woman's dignity and irreplaceable mission are greatly emphasized. Together with the man she is the minister of the sacrament of Marriage (n. 1623), and from that sacrament she receives the grace to love "with a supernatural love that is sensitive and fruitful" (n. 1642) in the bond of indissolubility and chaste fidelity (cf. nn. 1643-1648) and in the generous willingness to welcome life and to care for her children (cf. nn. 1652-1653).

Furthermore, by her example of self-denial and active charity, woman—wife and mother—is called to make her family a "domestic church" in which God is known, honored, prayed to and witnessed to in a holy life. In this holy environment she exercises her baptismal priesthood, handing on and nourishing the faith in her children and giving them a Christian upbringing (cf. nn. 1656-1657; 2685).

Those who can say that they learned the faith of Mother Church at their own mother's knee know how important and decisive this is in giving direction to their lives. Often behind great saints there are holy mothers. Most often, however, they remain in the background or—like Mary—they act as a monstrance.

The *Catechism* does not fail to consider the great perils which today threaten the dignity of woman and thus the integrity of the family. When woman wanders from the way of the Lord she may disfigure the maternal face of God (cf. n. 239); she ceases to be an image of his loving tenderness and, rather than placing herself at the service of life, she rejects it in the name of an ill-conceived emancipation, as though maternity—with all the duties and sacrifices it entails—were a burden and enslavement rather than a gift and an honor.

Here then is the scourge of abortion (cf. n. 2271) and, next to it, many other temptations which can distract woman—as much as man—from her noble task and lead her on the road to perversion and self-destruction (cf. n. 2353). Such is not only the rejection of motherhood but also the pretext of producing children by manipulating the laws of nature (cf. nn. 2376-2378).

The consecrated woman

As if to neutralize the disastrous consequences of these rampant forms of desecrating life, the *charisma* of consecrated virginity also exists in the Church (cf. nn. 918-933). There are women who, through a special vocation beyond the natural level, offer themselves to God with an undivided heart and anticipate in time the eternal reality of the mystical marriage of Christ and his Church. The *Catechism* notes, quoting the rite of the consecration of virgins, that they are "the transcendent sign of the love of the Church for Christ, the eschatological image of the heavenly Bride and of the life to come" (n. 923).

Precisely because of their total dedication to God these women become universal mothers in the order of grace and by their presence they offer the Church and mankind, especially the most materially and spiritually poor and needy, an inexhaustible source of charity, tender compassion and consolation.

Like a spring of water, hidden but full of boundless spiritual life, is the presence of consecrated women in the monastic and contemplative life (cf. nn. 2687; 2691). Their radical separation from the world in order to live in God's presence in pure offering and unceasing prayer, makes them closer to all people and renders them, in a certain way, the soul of every other vocation or mission in the Church; this is so because prayer is the "living source" which nourishes faith and charity and makes their works bear fruit.

The *Catechism*, however briefly, has not failed to indicate among the guides of the spiritual life and the teachers of prayer, some women who, by sanctifying themselves in the silence of the cloister have enriched the Church with that "wisdom of the heart" which alone makes us appreciate God (cf. nn. 2558; 2704; 2709). Furthermore we are reminded that "in the catacombs the Church is often depicted as a woman in prayer with arms open, raised in prayer . . . " (cf. n. 1368).

Perhaps this wonderful, touching image—and there are many of them living, visible or hidden—would be sufficient to erase all the deformed images of woman that mar the social environment and make "the world ugly" in the eyes of those who cannot see spiritual beauty: the consoling beauty which is the reflection of the glory of God in the Blessed Virgin Mary and in souls in which the Church is the perpetually young virgin-bride-mother (cf. n. 2502).

Appendices

I

The Catechism of the Catholic Church in context

Cardinal Joseph Ratzinger
Prefect of the Congregation for the Doctrine of the Faith

Press conference presenting
the *Catechism of the Catholic Church* to the media
Wednesday, December 9, 1992

The French edition of the *Catechism of the Catholic Church* was presented to the public in Paris Nov. 16, and on Dec. 7 the Holy Father formally presented it to the Christian world. In the interim the Italian and Spanish editions have been made available; other translations will follow shortly. The official Latin text will appear later, thus it will also be able to take into consideration what the experience of translating it has brought out or could still suggest. For some time now this book has been the topic of public debate since several drafts were wholly or partially made known.

What has been written so far about the *Catechism* was for the most part rather one-sided. Thus it could seem that it was really a list of sins and that the Church wanted most of all to tell people what they could not do. Nevertheless, the curiosity, even the passion, with which this book became the subject of debate long before its publication, even outside Catholic Christian circles, is an extremely important phenomenon. In fact, even where the comments were less positive, one felt that people were in some way affected by this book, by its questions and answers. It clearly showed that the problem of what we must do as human beings, of how we should live our lives so that we and the world may become just, is the essential problem of our day, and basically of all ages.

After the fall of ideologies, the problem of man—the moral problem—is presented to today's context in a totally new way: What should we do? How does life become just? What can give us and the whole world a future which is worth living? Since the *Catechism* treats these questions, it is a book which interests many people, far beyond purely theological or ecclesial circles. It can especially arouse interest because it does not merely present some private opinion invented by somebody or other, but formulates the response that comes from the great communal experience of the Church of all ages. This experience, however, is due in turn to a cognitive event which has its roots beyond what is merely human and hands on a divine revelation, what people who were in contact with God himself could see and hear.

Christian morality based on doctrine of Creation

What I have said up to this point could give rise to the question: Is the *Catechism* really a book of morals? The answer is: yes it is, but it is something more. It deals with the human person, but in the conviction that the human question cannot be separated from the God-question. One does not really speak rightly of man without speaking of God as well. However, we cannot really speak correctly about God if he himself does not tell us who he is. Therefore the moral directives offered by the *Catechism* cannot be separated from what it says about God and the history of God with us.

The *Catechism* must be read as a whole. It would be an erroneous reading of the pages on morality if they were to be separated from their context, namely, from the profession of faith and the teaching on the sacraments and prayer. In fact, the Catechism's basic assertion about human nature is as follows: man is created in the image and likeness of God. Everything that is said about proper human conduct is based on this central perspective. It is the basis of human rights, which belong to the human person from conception to the last instant of life. No one can grant them to him, just as no one can deprive him of them; they are inherent in his nature. This is also the basis of human dignity, which is intangible in every person precisely because he is a person. Last, included in it we also find the unity and equality of human beings: all human beings are creatures of the one God, and therefore all have equal dignity, all are united to one another by a fraternal bond, and all are responsible for one another and called to love their neighbors, whoever they may be.

In the *Catechism* the question about man and the God-question are inseparably interwoven; everything that is said about our moral conduct can therefore be said only from God's viewpoint, from the viewpoint of that God revealed in Jesus Christ. Thus it also becomes evident that in this conception of morality we do not have just a collection of prohibitions, a list of sins. It always involves the question of how can I make my human existence upright? How can I succeed in life? On this the *Catechism* speaks quite clearly through St. Augustine's conception of morality, which is very simple in its basic formulation. During the troubled course of his life he was always faced with the same question: What will make me happy? Everyone asks this question; the need for happiness is part of our nature.

With the faith of the Church as its point of departure, the *Catechism* tells us that happiness can be had only with others, in responsibility for the whole of humanity. However, the communion of human beings with one another and responsibility toward others can in turn ultimately be had only in communion with God and in responsibility before God. In this sense morality is a teaching about what happiness is and how it can be found—obviously, however, we are talking about true happiness, not a selfish happiness, which is only a semblance of happiness.

Hence the essential response which the *Catechism* in turn gives, based on the Bible, based on the Church's faith, is a very simple one: for the human person happiness is love. In this sense the Catechism's morality is an instruction on what love is. In this regard it tells us that the essence of true love became visible in the person of Jesus Christ, in his words as well as in his life and death. It also tells us that the Ten Commandments are only an explanation of love's ways; that we read them correctly only if we read them in Jesus Christ. In this sense all the essential contents of the profession of faith are found in the moral part, and there they become praxis.

In fact, the Catechism's morality has its starting point in what the Creator has placed in the heart of every person: the need for happiness and love. Here we also clearly see what is meant by God's likeness: human beings are like God because they can love and are capable of truth. Moral behavior is therefore in the deepest sense of the word a behavior with creation as the standard. If Catholic moral tradition and—in line with it—the *Catechism* too speak of the nature of the human being, the natural law and behavior according to nature, it does not mean a supposed biologism but behavior that begins from what the Creator has placed in our being. As a consequence the heart of all morality is love, and by always following this direction we inevitably find ourselves encountering Christ, the love of God made man.

Catechism structured according to Apostles' creed

I have dwelt a long time on how the moral question is presented in the *Catechism*, not to isolate morality again but rather, on the contrary, to arouse your interest in the *Catechism* as a whole, even though that may not be your immediate interest. Please allow me to add a few brief ideas about the remaining parts and some details of the Catechism's structure. As baptismal catechesis has done since the remotest times, the First Part follows the profession of faith, the so-called Apostle's Creed. During the first centuries this was the baptismal confession of the Church in Rome, and from Rome it became the norm for all of Western Christianity.

However, in its essential structure and its statements it corresponds perfectly with the Eastern baptismal confessions; the fact that we chose it as the *leit motif* for the *Catechism* should not, however, be seen as a unilateral preference for Western tradition.

A tradition dating back to the fourth century divides the creed into 12 articles in honor of the 12 apostles. This subdivision certainly has a valid sense, but the original structure is simpler: as a baptismal confession, the apostolic *Symbolum,* like the baptismal formula, is also quite simply a profession of faith in the Triune God, Father, Son and Holy Spirit. We retained this triple structure, which is common to all baptismal professions. Thus we see quite well the hierarchy of truths: At base the Christian faith is simply faith in God; all the rest is development. Our faith is not a theory but an event, an encounter with the living God, who is our Father, who welcomed human nature in his Son Jesus Christ and who unites us in the Holy Spirit, and in all this remains the one and only God. Through the link between the teaching of the faith and the baptismal profession it also becomes very clear that catechesis is not merely a communication of religious theory but is meant to begin a vital process: entrance into communion with God through baptism.

Thus we quite naturally move to the Second Part in which the seven sacraments are presented. The sacraments are the Church in her realization. The history of all religions recognizes sacred signs. The human being can enter into contact with the eternal only by means of the tangible, but the things of this world also have a certain internal predisposition to mediate contact with God. In this way the signs of creation and the symbolic world prepared by various religions could be taken up by the faith and, following Christ's mandate, become signs of redemption.

For this very reason we have always sought to present the sacraments beginning from their liturgical form. Therefore this Second Part is also an introduction to the Church's liturgy. Our difficulty was that in a book meant for the whole Church we could not begin with a single rite, for example the Latin one, as a starting point. Concrete explanations of individual rites must at times be made in catechesis. We were concerned to emphasize the common fundamental structure of the various rites. That was not always easy to do, but it became a fascinating task: now it can be seen how in the great diversity of liturgical forms there are still important common symbols, and thus they clearly show the will of Christ himself.

Commentary on Our Father

The Fourth Part, which deals with prayer, in some way summarizes the parts that preceded it: prayer is applied faith. It is inseparably united with the sacramental world. Sacraments predispose one to personal prayer, and in turn they alone give personal prayer a solid orientation in that they insert it into the Church's common prayer and, therefore, into Christ's dialogue with the Father. However, prayer and morality are also inseparable: It is only through conversion to God that the ways of true human fulfillment are opened. It is from prayer that we continually receive the necessary correction; through reconciliation with God it becomes possible to be reconciled with each other.

Along the lines of the great catechetical traditions, the *Catechism* gives in the section on prayer, which in substance is a commentary on the Our Father, a further meaning: prayer is an expression of our hope. The fact that we pray, that we have to ask, shows that our life and the world are imperfect; they are in need of help from on high. The fact that we are allowed to pray and that we are able to pray shows that we have been given the gift of a hope which is summarized in the invocation: "thy kingdom come."

When we say these words we pray for the present world, but at the same time we are praying for eternal life, for the new world. Thus in the four parts of the *Catechism* we see the mutual integration of faith, hope and charity. From the very moment we believe, we are allowed to hope. Because we believe and hope, we are capable of loving.

In conclusion, please let me give a few practical guidelines for reading the book. Historical notes and complementary doctrinal expositions are printed in small type and can even be omitted by readers who are less interested in a specialized viewpoint. However, we also printed in small type a rather large number of brief, poignant texts taken from the fathers, the liturgy, the Magisterium and Church history, which should help the reader understand something of the richness of the faith and its beauty. In this regard we took pains to present a balanced witness from the East and the West in order to illustrate the truly Catholic nature of the *Catechism*; we also sought to include the words of holy women. The catechetical nature of the book is clearly seen in the so-called "*En bref*" that are found at the end of every thematic section. The *Catechism* itself explains that their purpose is to offer suggestions for local catechesis in drafting summary statements that can be memorized (n. 22).

Naturally, we could say much more, for example, on the ecumenical nature of the book, on its relation to local catechisms, on concrete catechetical work and much more. However, all this must be left to further reflection on the *Catechism*; besides, much by way of explanation in this regard has already been said. My explanation was meant to be merely an invitation to read it and offer some help in beginning this reading. In conclusion I would like to read the words with which the preface to the *Catechism* ends, which in turn are from the preface to the *Catechism* of Trent.

"All the substance of doctrine and teaching must be oriented toward charity, which will never pass away. In fact, whether one is explaining the truths of faith, or the reasons for hope, or the duties of moral conduct, always and in everything emphasis should be given to the love of our Lord so as to help people understand that every exercise of perfect Christian virtue can flow from nothing other than love, just as in love it also has its ultimate goal" (n. 25 of the *Roman Catechism*, Preface 10).

II

'Catechism of the Catholic Church' must serve as a model and exemplar for local catechisms

Archbishop Crescenzio Sepe
Secretary of the Congregation for the Clergy

Reports (conclusions) on the Seminar
on the *Catechism of the Catholic Church*
and the catechetical apostolate
April 29, 1993

1. First of all, I want to offer a word of gratitude and appreciation for your having overcome a number of difficulties in order to come here from five continents, for the commitment you put into the work, and for the atmosphere of communion and cordial fraternity we have experienced together.

2. During these three days we have made a very thorough study of the relationship between the *Catechism of the Catholic Church* and the *catechetical apostolate*.

3. We considered the main points of this relationship, in particular the way in which, as a reference point, the *Catechism of the Catholic Church* must be used in a catechesis that responds to the demands of an authentic transmission of the faith and inculturated in diocesan and national catechisms which will be effective instruments for the new evangelization.

4. We listened with particular attention and deep interest to the reports of Fr. Georges Cottier who spoke on "Unity of Faith and Pluralism of Culture", and to Cardinal Francis Arinze, who developed the topic "In what way can the *Catechism of the Catholic Church* be a sure and authentic reference text in preparing local catechisms?."

5. The *overview* of the use of the *Catechism* on the six continents, offered by Archbishops Legaspi and Stroba and by Bishops Bududira, Camacho, Leibrecht, and Villalba, was very interesting. The testimony emerging from the interventions presented not only demands open questions and points for research, but also positive data and concrete prospects for the future. These interventions ranged from Ireland to Australia, from Canada to Thailand, from Slovakia to Madagascar, in a truly universal perspective.

6. This wealth of contributions was further deepened in the study groups whose reflections were summarized in reports presented by the moderators.

The following are summaries of the conclusions they reached:

7. Characteristics shared in common

- *The 'Catechism of the Catholic Church' is an 'ecclesial event'*

  The very positive reception being given the *Catechism of the Catholic Church* shows that it is not just one more text, but rather an *ecclesial event* rich in consequences for the life and apostolate of the ecclesial communities. It is considered as a great *Catechism* which shows Mother Church prophetically in dialogue with the world. Through it the Church speaks a single language. As an ecclesial event, the *Catechism* commits the whole Church to feeling responsible for courageously and faithfully presenting her own doctrine.

- *The 'Catechism of the Catholic Church' is an instrument of communion*

  A basic attitude, one which precedes all others, for the proper use of the *Catechism of the Catholic Church is* recognizing it as an act of the Petrine Magisterium and the College of Bishops, to be understood, however, not as a merely juridical gesture, but as a "precious gift" from Mother Church, which deserves to be given loyal acceptance, intelligent comprehension and responsible commitment to pursue the objective which the *Catechism* sets in advance.

The *Catechism of the Catholic Church* has made possible the unification of multiple national programs for catechesis. Non Catholics, and even non Christians too, can find in the document a sure way of knowing the Catholic faith and therefore an instrument of ecumenism and dialogue as well.

- **The *'Catechism of the Catholic Church'* is a reference point**

  It is a reference point in the sense that in its teaching it is normative for all future activity because of its thoroughness and authoritativeness.

It is important to specify that *reference point* should be *understood in its strongest sense,* that is, that the *Catechism of the Catholic Church* is not just any text but a magisterial text which, because it is a model and exemplar, is:

—a sure norm for teaching and living the faith and Catholic doctrine;

—a sure, authentic text for preparing local catechisms.

In this regard the Holy Father said during the audience on April 29: "This *Catechism* is also the 'type' and 'exemplar' for other catechisms, a sure reference text for teaching Catholic doctrine and in a very special way for drafting local catechisms. It cannot be considered merely as a stage preceding the drafting of local catechisms, but is destined for all the faithful who have the capacity to read, understand and assimilate it in their Christian living. In this perspective it becomes the support and foundation for the preparation of new catechetical tools which take the cultural situations into consideration and together take pains to preserve the unit of the faith and fidelity to Catholic doctrine (cf. *Fidei Depositum,* n. 4)."

Since it is a point of reference the Catechism's influence must be felt in three interrelated fields, namely, catechesis, catechists and catechisms.

◘ *Concerning catechesis*

In the complex process of the renewal of catechesis begun with Vatican II, it is both a point of arrival and a point of departure.

However, in regard to catechesis its basic achievements (which also become criteria for evaluation) concern:

—contents

—the nature of catechesis

—the dimensions of catechesis

—pedagogical authority

◘ *Concerning catechisms*

No local catechism can contain any element which is or may be interpreted as contrary to the teaching of the *Catechism of the Catholic Church*. Local cultural mentalities could determine their approach, style, formulas to be used, etc.

The concrete manner of presentation will be characterized by the groups to which it is directed: the community of believers, post-Christian society, or those who have not yet received the message of the Gospel.

The four-part structure of the *Catechism of the Catholic Church* is to be highly recommended.

Wherever it is not possible to create a national catechism, the *Catechism of the Catholic Church* itself can become the national catechism.

Some authoritative and normative data stemming from the very nature of the *Catechism of the Catholic Church* must be firmly established. Some criteria can be offered as an example:

—sure, authoritative doctrinal reference;

—a model for a first level of inculturation that combines the essential and organic with the cultural context;

—ecumenical perspective and missionary activity;

—the nature of the people and the different educational processes.

◘ *Concerning catechists*

Because catechists are both the agents and recipients of catechesis and the use of the text, it is necessary that they have a first-hand knowledge of the *Catechism of the Catholic Church* and assimilate its theological significance and magisterial relevance. In this sense the *Catechism of the Catholic Church* can be an instrument for the ongoing formation of the members of the Church, namely:

—*Bishops,* as the primary recipients of the *Catechism of the Catholic Church* and those primarily responsible for the formation of catechists;

—*Priests,* in their ongoing formation and preaching;

—*Catechists* in their specific preparation for the service of the Word;

—*Theologians,* as a reference point for orthodoxy of doctrine and fidelity in teaching;

—*Seminarians* in their formation process;

—*All the faithful* who have the capacity to read it, understand it, and assimilate it in their Christian living.

The '*Catechism* of the Catholic Church' and inculturation

8. The principal factor of inculturation is the catechist. It is necessary to focus on the formation of priests, religious and lay catechists who, nourished by the *Catechism of the Catholic Church,* will be intelligent and faithful agents in the work of inculturation.

Another factor of inculturation is the local catechisms. They must show creativity in fidelity; they should devise ways to inculturate the manner in which the faith is passed on and taught to the people of every cultural and social context.

It is important that inculturation does not become an artificial methodology, or otherwise it would risk denying the mystery of the incarnation, a unique event, as exemplary as it is singular, for every inculturation.

A lengthy work of inculturation is required for the cultural areas of Africa (ancestral religions), the Arab world (interreligious dialogue, war and peace . . .) and the Latin-American cultures (ancestral religions).

Open perspectives

9. From the individual groups some problems and difficulties emerged which can also be summarized so that everyone may feel encouraged to respond to them according to his abilities.

Quite a few Churches suffer from a severe lack of personnel, resources and structures; they suffer from problems due to linguistic differences, geographical distances, or their minority status compared to other Christian communities or other religions.

In this perspective the Bishops of Eastern Europe appealed for aid, which the Church in Russia especially needs, since it has suffered more than other countries in the area of catechetical ministry.

We all feel touched by these and many other types of need which, coming from other Churches too, appeal to our solidarity.

The meeting with the Pope

10. Our meeting with the Pope was a source of comfort, support and encouragement for all. His words will serve as light and guidance for this new, promising phase of work which awaits the Congregation and the Episcopates of the world.

Conclusion and hopes

11. The Congregation for the Clergy will evaluate and study everything. None of the valuable contributions of these days will be lost. Obviously there is a need for a suitable period of time to make a proper discernment together with the other dicasteries involved.

The Congregation intends to present everything to the Holy Father and then bring it to the attention of the whole Episcopate.

We entrust the results of our work to Christ the Teacher and to the Virgin Mary, the "Star of Evangelization", so that the *depositum fidei,* the unity of truth, and communion in the Church may be preserved and faithfully transmitted in the process of the new evangelization.

Index